The Sublime Treasures

Answers to Sufi Questions

The Sublime Treasures

Answers to Sufi Questions

By

Imām
'Abdallāh al-Ḥaddād

Translated by

Moṣṭafā al-Badawī

FONS VITAE

First published in 2008 by
Fons Vitae
49 Mockingbird Valley Drive
Louisville, KY 40207
http://www.fonsvitae.com
Email: fonsvitaeky@aol.com

Library of Congress Control Number: 2007942151
ISBN 1-887752-34-X

Printed in Canada

The author of this book, Imām 'Abdallāh 'Alawī al-Ḥaddād (died, 1720), was one of the most illustrious masters of the house of Banī 'Alawī, the descendants of Imām Ḥusayn who settled in Hadramawt, and is widely held to have been the spiritual "renewer" of the twelfth Islāmic century. That Imām al-Ḥaddād was the ultimate authority of his time, especially as concerns questions of method and gnosis, is substantiated by the statements of the saints of his time. A direct descendant of the Prophet, his sanctity and direct experience of God are clearly reflected in his writings.

Other Fons Vitae titles in the
Imām al-Ḥaddād Spiritual Master series include:

The Lives of Man (1991)
The Book of Assistance (2003)
Gifts for the Seeker (2003)
The Sufi Sage of Arabia (2005)

This book was typeset by Neville Blakemore, Jr

CONTENTS

Translator's Introduction

In the Name of God, the All-Merciful, the Compassionate

As one meditates upon the verses of the Qur'ān, one notices how repeatedly it stresses that for humankind a path is open which leads to the Divine Presence. Verses such as the following clearly express this: "*This is indeed a Reminder; so he who will, takes unto his Lord a way.*" [76:29] This way is the Straight Path: "*Say: To God belong the East and the West; He guides whomsoever He will to a straight path.*" [2:142] "*And We elected them, and We guided them to a straight path.*" [6:87] The first mention of the Straight Path in the Qur'ān comes in the *Fātiḥa*, the prayer that every Muslim repeats at least seventeen times a day: "*Guide us to the straight path.*" [1:6] It is remarkable that in the *Fātiḥa* the Straight Path is defined as: "*The path of those whom You have favored*" [1:7], defined, that is, in terms of those who follow it. The verse does not say: "follow the path of God!" although the Qur'ān speaks in similar terms elsewhere, but it says: "*The path of those whom You have favored.*" Those human beings which are described further on as: "*Those that God has favored: the Prophets, the Ṣiddīqūn,*[1] *the Martyrs and the virtuous.*" [4:69] The Path is defined in terms of those who follow it in the most perfect manner, the four categories stated in this verse, a clear reference to the necessity for spiritual guidance and a command for the rest of the believers to follow the example and guidance of the masters[2], those whom God has favored with the knowledge of Revelation: "*Then We bequeathed the Book on those of Our servants We chose.*" [35:32]

The believer who decides to embark on a serious quest for the Truth will meet with numerous perplexities and intriguing questions. As with any other discipline, the more the novice advances the more questions arise concerning both theory and practice. The difference between Sufism and other disciplines is that, in addition to theoretical knowledge and practical experience, it requires the inward realization of the spiritual stations leading to gnosis, which is the direct knowledge of the contemplative,[3] the final aim of *ṭarīqa* (spiritual method).

The master best capable of answering questions on Sufism with authority should therefore be one in full possession of the three conditions of being well steeped in the theoretical knowledge of all branches of *sharī'a* (sacred law), experienced in the practice of *ṭarīqa*, and of having received from God the realization of a high spiritual rank.

The author of this volume, Imām 'Abdallāh ibn 'Alawī al-Ḥaddād (may God be pleased with him) was one of the most illustrious masters of the house of Banī 'Alawī, the descendants of Imām Ḥusayn who settled in Hadramawt. His destiny was to be the one upon whom fell the necessary burden of reformulating the 'Alawī method and shaping it into the form it is to retain until the end of time.

The 'Alawī *ṭarīqa* is the *ṭarīqa* of *Ahl al-Bayt* (members of the Prophet's House) par excellence. This is not to say that other *ṭarīqas* are not, since most Sufi masters are of either Ḥasanī or Ḥusaynī descent, but that the 'Alawīs are to this day so permeated with the original spirit of *Ahl al-Bayt* that it is impossible to mention either without recalling the other. The fact that the *ṭarīqa* is transmitted by one generation of masters after another rather than by single chains and that most of the disciples are themselves *sharīfs* reinforces this quality so much so that they are referred to simply as *al-sāda*. They are firmly entrenched[4] in the Book of God and *Sunna* of His Messenger, avoiding all special techniques and practices not explicitly stated in them. This is how Imām Aḥmad ibn Zayn al-Ḥabashī[5] could say: "We give no words priority over those of our master and shaykh 'Abdallāh, except for the Book of God and *Sunna* of His Messenger, for the meanings of these have taken deep roots in his heart and permeated his secret (*sirr*), so much so that they have become the source from whence spring his words."

Being so thoroughly that of *Ahl al-Bayt*, the 'Alawī *ṭarīqa* is seen to be remarkably universal, open and tolerant of all other *ṭarīqas*. They never claim to be better than others and always adopt a gentle, unassuming manner.

Shaykh Shihāb al-Dīn Aḥmad al-Tumbuktī,[6] who lived in Madina, taught in the Prophet's mosque and met Imām al-Ḥaddād during his *Ḥajj*, said: "I was very attached to my master Shaykh 'Abdal-Qādir al-Jīlānī and he used to appear to me openly. When I became attached to my master 'Abdallāh al-Ḥaddād and became soundly affiliated with him, I no longer saw Shaykh 'Abdal-Qādir. When this reached my master 'Abdallāh he remarked: 'Shaykh 'Abdal-Qādir is to us as a father.' It was as if he had said: 'We and he are one, when one of us is not there the other stands in for him,' and God knows best."

The Imām repeatedly stated that Shaykh 'Abdal-Qādir was one of his four closest spiritual mentors, whose spiritual influence he received from the other-world. The 'Alawīs also received the powerful spiritual influence of the chain of Shaykh Abū Madyan, the spiritual ancestor of the Shādhilīs and other *ṭarīqas*. This chain includes Imām al-Ghazālī as well as the Master of the Faction,[7] Shaykh al-Junayd and his chain of spiritual masters up to Shaykh al-Ḥasan al-Baṣrī, Imām 'Alī's disciple. The universality of the 'Alawīs is further shown by the fact that they recommend the recitation of the *awrād* and *aḥzāb* of Imām Abul-Ḥasan al-Shādhilī, Imām al-Nawawī, and other masters, in addition to their own.

The 'Alawīs always insist on their disciples acquiring the knowledge of the numerous sciences of *sharī'a* from whichever teacher God places on their path. They do not mind their attending sessions of *dhikr* with other *ṭarīqas*, unless these involve something forbidden or *makrūh*, and it is unheard of for an 'Alawī master to restrain his disciples from visiting other shaykhs and partaking of their *baraka*. This gives the 'Alawīs a broad perspective and, coupled with their constant endeavor to make the Prophetic knowledge intelligible to the majority of Muslims, their willingness to teach and look after disciples of knowledge from any *ṭarīqa*, and their total disregard for artificial boundaries and narrow sectarianism makes them exemplary teachers. Intelligibility is indeed the major attribute of Imām al-Ḥaddād's works. This book, however, is a little different. Here the disciple with a restless mind and countless unanswered questions will find information presented in the Imām's inimitable style of succinct clarity. There are answers to questions pertaining exclusively to Sufism such as those concerning the Pole of the Time and the Circle of Saints, the *Afrād*, who are the solitary saints said by some to be outside the jurisdiction of the Pole and in direct contact with al-Khidr,[8] the definition of the *ṣiddīq*, that of the *majdhūb*, the states of extinction and subsistence, various technical points concerning the relationship between the master and the novice, Sufi courtesy with God and His saints, the worlds of *Mulk*, *Malakūt*, *Jabarūt* and *Lāhūt*, which are the degrees of universal existence, and how to deal with obscure passages in the works of such esoteric writers as Ibn 'Arabī. There are also questions of a more general tenor such as those concerning the degrees of the Garden and its gates, the merits of the recitation of the Qur'ān over *awrād*, the respective merits and courtesies of poverty and wealth, and of fame and obscurity, the faith of the *muqallid*, the offering of the rewards of certain acts of worship to the spirits of the dead, the signs of the *du'ā'* that is answered, sins committed in *Ramaḍān* when the devils are shackled, and the causes of the civil wars that 'Alī ibn Abī-Ṭālib was forced to wage.

It will easily be noticed how the Imām curtly sweeps aside anything that has no direct bearing on the traveler's path. Questions devoid of practical value are pitilessly dismissed in a summary manner and the reader is firmly reoriented to what is of immediate benefit to him. The 'Alawīs in general and Imām al-Ḥaddād in particular have always been most reluctant to discourse openly on Divine secrets, knowing that such discourse causes much confusion and frequently leads novices into believing or pretending they have reached degrees and states which they have not. The Imām allowed himself more freedom in letters addressed to his scholarly disciples—extracts of which constitute this volume—than in books. He also expressed in his *Dīwān* of poems much that he refrains from saying in his books. He once wrote to Shaykh Bā-'Abbād: "You say your desire was not fulfilled by what we wrote concerning the words of Imām al-Ghazālī in *"Kimiā' [al-Sa'āda]"* (The Alchemy of Happiness). The thing is that this is all that came to mind, there are limits which we cannot exceed in books in these times. However, if you meditate on it thoroughly the problem will be resolved entirely." Further on in the same letter he says: "We allow during our discourses and conversations some of this knowledge [to come out], even though it is subtle and needs much elaboration, but we allow none of that in our books or letters. Discourses are understood by those qualified to understand, as for those who are not, they represent simply accidental events, things which pass them by, leaving them with nothing in their hands.[9] This is some of the support that God grants the people of this faction. It is not the same for what is written on paper, it is exposed to the good and the corrupt, so do understand!"

As for his private conversations with other gnostics, these have remained secret to this day. Among those were his long sessions with Imām Aḥmad ibn Zayn al-Ḥabashī on the famous staircase landing in his house at al-Ḥāwī. When Imām Aḥmad ibn Zayn asked him why he was not better known to the people, he answered: "You should thank God for that, for otherwise you and I would never have had the opportunity to sit together like that."

That Imām al-Ḥaddād was the ultimate authority of his time, especially as concerns questions of method and gnosis, is substantiated by the statements of the saints of his time. Shaykh al-Tumbuktī wrote to him from Madina in the following terms: "May God preserve the Pole of the time, the cave of splendor and shade, the exemplar of the people of perfection, the fountain of the people of solicitude,[10] the divine gnostic, the reviver of the practices of *Ṭarīqa* and *Ḥaqīqa*, the unveiler of subtle secrets, the one who is an ocean from the current of which gnostics scoop, a lamp the lights of which are sought by those who know God. From the [zodiacal] sign of his gnosis rise the planets of solicitude. The meadows of nearness unfurl the banners of election for him. Detachment remained his inner garment, circumspection his cloak, remembrance his intimate comfort, reflection his companion, until the veiled secrets appeared to him, the hidden realities manifested to him from behind the veils, and the realities of the life-to-come were unveiled for him in this life. His glory has deep roots and his eminence high peaks. Leadership is his by right and mastery his firm possession. He is the master of the noblemen (*sharīfs*), the manifestation of [the essence of] existence, the chosen one from the House of Manāf, the one selected to receive the solicitude of the Lord of men, our master and patron 'Abdallāh ibn 'Alawī al-Ḥaddād, may God spread his benefit!"

Imām al-Ḥaddād himself once stated that he was in possession of sciences which he could reveal to none for fear of their being denied, even by scholars. When asked by

Imām Aḥmad al-Ḥabashī about the question of individual responsibility as posed in the science of principles,[11] he answered: "O Aḥmad! God has revealed to me the fountainheads of truth and I have seen the principles of the exponents of [the science of] principles. This question is one of taste. The reality of its truth will become unveiled only in the life-to-come." On certain occasions when he discoursed on essential realities and Divine secrets that not one of the people in attendance was able to grasp, he remarked that there were men from the unseen (*rijāl al-ghayb*) present to receive his discourse. He sometimes added: "Our sessions are not exclusively yours; they also involve other of God's created beings, men, jinn, and men of the unseen. Those of them whom God wishes are enabled to attend."

Most of the questions in the book were forwarded to the Imām by scholars and experienced travelers on the Sufi path. The answers therefore presume a substantial amount of knowledge in the questioner and then build upon that. This sometimes makes it difficult for those without a similar background to follow the argumentation or to understand allusions to concepts, elaborate scholarly arguments, and events which the Imām takes for granted as already familiar to the reader. This is the main reason why this book should be read either in the presence or under the supervision of an authorized shaykh. Unlike other Sufi writing, there is little danger of the Imām's intentions being misunderstood, since he consistently maintains extreme circumspection and is always keen to avoid such risks. However, because of the above mentioned reasons, some meanings may be understood less than fully, others missed altogether.

These answers were gleaned from the Imām's correspondence at his bidding by Imām Aḥmad ibn Zayn al-Ḥabashī. He omitted the customary opening and concluding formulae, as well as all references to personal matters, retaining only those parts of the letters that had a doctrinal content. In the original manuscript as well as the printed Cairo edition of 1982 there were no numbers to the questions. We followed the numeration of the Beirut edition of 1993, although not entirely satisfactory, and added some notes, though much fewer than the text requires in order to become fully intelligible without recourse to a qualified teacher. We also omitted the formulae used by Imām al-Ḥabashī to introduce each answer, such as: "He answered—may God the Exalted be pleased with him and reward him well," "He answered him—may God be pleased with him and give us of his spiritual assistance!" or "He answered him—may God increase him in merit and give us of his *baraka*!" and so on.

Contrary to the other works of Imām al-Ḥaddād, the translation of this material required much clarification, which was provided by the late Ḥabīb Aḥmad Mashhūr al-Ḥaddād (may God be pleased with him), who, until his death on the 6th of December 1995, had been the foremost authority on Imām al-Ḥaddād's works. May God sanctify their secrets and reward them for what they have accomplished for Islam and Muslims in general and for us, their disciples and servants, in particular. May God bless our master Muḥammad, the perfection of His grace, his noble illustrious family, knowledgeable rightly guiding Companions, and descendants of the House of al-Ḥaddād, and may He bless us along with them, with a blessing such as to make us reach our ultimate desire; may God whelm us along with them with peace such as to give us firm mastery, and may these blessings and peace endure till the day we meet Him in their company. Amen!

Imām
'Abdallāh al-Ḥaddād

The Sublime Treasures

Answers to Sufi Questions

THE SUBLIME TREASURES
ANSWERS TO SUFI QUESTIONS

In the Name of God, the All-Merciful,

the Compassionate.

In Him I trust.

All praise belongs to God, the One, the Unique, the First, the Last, the Supreme, the Independent, the Designer, the Generous, the Munificent, Whose marvelous creations are endless and Whose gifts flow in streams innumerable. It is Him that I praise and thank as befits His favors and equals His liberality; and it is Him that I ask for success in pleasing Him and for security under His protection and support.

I testify that there is no divinity other than God, alone, with no partners, a testimony such as to place me in the wake of those whose [spiritual] states are true, whose souls are serene, and whose doctrine is correct. And I testify that our lord Muḥammad, the unlettered Prophet, is His servant and messenger, with whom the pure law and the straight path were sent forth and established on their foundations. He is perfect, and he perfects those of his praiseworthy community who emulate him. May God bestow upon him blessings and peace as perpetual as time itself, and upon his family and companions who are the very treasuries of sciences, the ascending stars, the lordly warriors [whose assistance is provided] in the hardest times. And [may the same blessings and peace be] upon all those who follow their guidance and in their footsteps, who are heirs to their pattern of wisdom, particularly those who, having elevated themselves, attained to lofty ranks, and acquired the realities that are the consequence of emulation, who became known as the Sufi masters, more especially those who are noble by birth as well as by their manifest succession to the said [spiritual] states, ranks, and praiseworthy conduct, by whom I mean the Ḥusaynī *sayyids* of penetrating *karāmāt*, dazzling proofs, and Muḥammadan behavior, and in particular the light of their eyes, the one whose *baraka* envelops the whole world, whose sciences shine through his words to dazzle the mind, the Shaykh of Islam, the Muḥammadan Heir immersed in the solicitude of God the Generous and Liberal, our shaykh and our blessing, 'Abdallāh ibn 'Alawī ibn Muḥammad ibn Aḥmad ibn 'Abdallāh al-Ḥaddād Bā-'Alawī, the Ḥusaynī, the Ash'arī.

May God grant us of his spiritual support (*madad*) and prolong it so as to delight all Muslims. O God! Bless Your Prophet Muḥammad and his descendants, and align me with them! Grant me the realization of their knowledge, together with perfect health and safety, until such time as I meet You in the manner that most pleases You, and grant the same to my parents and teachers, O God, O Most Merciful.

These are "The Sublime Treasures on Sufi Questions," the opinions of our Shaykh, the noble *sayyid* 'Abdallāh ibn 'Alawī. He bid me collect them and he gave them their lofty title.

May God the Generous accept!

We shall now begin:

1

> The noble *sayyid* of sublime excellence, Abū-Bakr, son of *sayyid* Shaykh al-Saqqāf Bā-'Alawī asked Imām al-Ḥaddād: "What do you say of such thoughts as occur to one who has reached God the Exalted? Should he reject them and depend solely on thoughts of divine origin or should he do otherwise?"

His answer was: The one who has arrived to God the Exalted is the one who has reached the limit, in his knowledge of God the Transcendent and Exalted that any person of knowledge can reach. Men of this rank differ to an incalculable extent and they are in either one of two states: union (*jam*') or separation (*farq*). When the state of union comes upon one of them he becomes extinct to himself and to others and absorbed in his Lord, [to the extent of being] totally annihilated in Him. At such a time no thoughts occur and nothing that exists is perceived; only the One whose existence is real, Transcendent and Majestic be He! A man who had realized this state once described it thus:

> If ever a wish for any other than You should cross my
> mind
> Out of distraction I would declare myself an apostate.

Which means: I would declare myself not to be totally absorbed and annihilated in You. And God knows best.

Another has said:

> In my heart there used to be different passions
> But all passions became one as soon as the eye
> beheld You.

Thoughts and their ramifications are the result of worries and the multiplicity of attachments. Those who have reached God the Exalted suffer from none of these, for they have united all their anxious desires into only one, which is God the Exalted!

It is to union that this saying of the Prophet (may God's blessings and peace be upon him) refers: "I have a time when only my Lord can fill me."

The perpetuation of the state of union is extremely rare, but when it is sustained strange and wondrous things occur. A shaykh in Iraq remained in this state for seven years, he then came to for a brief period, then returned to it for a further seven years. During the whole of that period he never ate, drank, slept, or prayed, but just stood there in the desert gazing at heaven. Another shaykh in Egypt is said to have once made his ritual ablutions (*wuḍū*'), laid down and instructed his deputy not to awaken him, but to let him awake of his own accord. Seventeen years elapsed during which he remained asleep, finally he awoke and stood up for prayers without repeating his ritual ablutions.

Gnostics (*'ārifūn*) yearn for union, but the Real, out of compassion, moves them out of it, that they may fulfill their obligations, that their bodies may not waste nor their bones wither away. For when the manifestations of the higher worlds (*wāridāt*) descend and are powerful and overwhelming, they cannot be sustained by human powers; and how could they be so when even Mount Sinai was consumed and reduced to dust when that Light appeared to it?[12]

A claim of union is unacceptable from those people who have come under the devil's sway, abandoned acts of worship, neglected such obligations as prayers and fasts, indulged their lustful desires and committed forbidden acts. Had they [truly] been saints of God the Exalted (*awliyā'*) He would have protected them [from such behavior]; and had they been absorbed in Him, they would have lost awareness of all else.

We should not prolong our discussion of this matter even though it is a vast one where many a foot has slipped, for it is a thing to be experienced and is difficult for the mind[13], let alone the imagination[14], to grasp.

As for the state of separation, he who reaches God is preserved therein by the eye of divine solicitude. There only thoughts of Lordly origin occur, which the Sufis call 'permission' (*idhn*) and thoughts of angelic origin, which they call 'inspiration' (*ilhām*). Only the Book and *Sunna* take precedence over such thoughts.

As for satanic thoughts, they no longer occur, for the 'Repudiate' cannot come near the hearts of those who have reached God the Exalted and become illumined with the lights of gnosis (*ma'rifa*).[15] Their devils may even become Muslims, an occurrence which falls into the pattern inherited from their Prophet (may God's blessings and peace be upon him) for he has said: "I have a devil, but God, Transcendent and Exalted is He, assisted me against him until he became a Muslim and he now enjoins nothing but good." Thoughts arising from the soul (*nafs*) are a remote possibility, for the soul of one who has reached God is serene in its Lord, has reached His proximity and is conforming and obedient. Called by its Lord, it has answered, so He made it join His servants in a "*Garden the breadth of which is the heavens and the earth, which was prepared for those who fear God.*" [3:133]

2

Sayyid Shaykh al-Saqqāf also asked him about the sins of the gnostics.

He replied: In Sufi terminology a gnostic (*'ārif*) is a person who believes in God in full awareness, learns about those obligations and prohibitions which God has imposed upon him, obeys them, then increasingly performs supererogatory devotions which draw him nearer to God, Exalted is He, seeking His proximity, until the lights of good fortune dawn upon him, the unseen becomes to him as the seen, and the Real guides him to His path, grants him discernment and teaches him directly of His own knowledge.

It is possible for the gnostic who has reached this degree to commit a sin and it is possible for him from both the rational and the legal points of view to receive punishment for it. The maximum for a gnostic is to be a saint (*walī*) and the maximum for a saint is to be guarded [from sins].

There is no doubt that some of the Prophets (may God's blessings and peace be upon them all) were indeed reproached for things they had done. So it was in that which happened to Adam (may God's blessings and peace be upon our Prophet and him), when he ate from the tree; to David (may God's blessings and peace be upon our Prophet and upon him), when he looked that look and had that thought; and to Solomon (may God's blessings and peace be upon our Prophet and him), when he felt that inclination, not one atom of which was converted into action. However, the majority of scholars are of the opinion that all Prophets (may God's blessings and peace be upon them all) are totally immune from both major and minor sins and that those things which some committed were but mistakes and omissions.

It is well recognized and confirmed that the good works of the gnostics attract more reward than those of others and are subjected to multiplication, and so also their sins, for reproaches will be greater and retribution more severe. They may thus receive for a minor misdemeanor the same punishment that others receive for a major one; and that is because they are within the enclosure of [divine] proximity. Have you not heard His saying, Exalted is He: "*O wives of the Prophet! Those of you who commit an evident indecency, her punishment shall be doubled, that is easy for God, but those of you who obey God and His Messenger, and behave well, We shall pay her reward twice over.*" [33:30-31]

It has reached us that the gnostic, Ibn al-Jalā' (may God's mercy be upon him) once glanced at a good looking beardless youth, and it was said to him: "You will meet with the consequence, even if after some time!" He later forgot the Qur'ān [which he had memorized]. Another had a sinful thought while praying and his whole body turned black and remained so until a certain scholar of authority interceded on his behalf. As for al-Junayd, he saw a poor man begging and thought: "Would it not be better for this one to work for his living?" When he rose to his night devotions he found himself lacking in energy and unable to enjoy them; he was then overcome by sleep and saw that the beggar in question had been brought and laid before him. He was told: "Eat of his flesh for you have slandered him!" He said: "Transcendent is God! It was but a thought!" And he was told: "For such a one as you it is not permissible." Others were punished for things they had done which were in themselves licit but were lacking the courtesy appropriate to their rank. Such was what happened to Abū-Turāb al-Nakhshabī (may God's mercy be upon him) when he felt a desire for bread and eggs and entered a town to indulge his wish. One of the townsmen took hold of him and cried: "This man was with the thieves!" Thus it was that he received a painful beating until a man recognized him, took him to his house and there offered him that which had been his desire, at which [Abū-Turāb] addressed his soul thus: "Eat! After so many blows!" Yet another who had resolved never to eat fish was overcome by his ego, reached for it and his hand was penetrated by a fishbone which ruined it. It has also reached us that Shaykh Abul-Ghayth (may God's mercy be upon him) once kissed his wife without first forming an [appropriate] intention and his rank was diminished for a full year. There are many more such stories but, God willing, those we have mentioned should suffice to make the point, while maintaining our intended brevity.

3

> The scholarly Shaykh, 'Abd al-Raḥmān al-Khatīb Bā-Rajā asked him whether the *Quṭb* was the same as the *Ghawth*, and about the *Awtād*, the *Abdāl*, and other men of God.

He answered: Know, my brother, that there are many *ḥadiths* attributed to the Messenger of God (may God's blessings and peace be upon him) concerning this matter, as well as many statements attributed to God the Exalted's elect. I shall confine myself to one *ḥadith* and a few of the other sayings. Al-Yāfi'ī (may God's mercy be upon him) wrote in "*Rawḍ al-Rayāḥīn*" (The Meadow of Fragrant Plants) that according to Ibn Mas'ūd (may God be pleased with him), the Messenger of God (may God's blessings and peace be upon him) said: "God the Exalted has on His earth three hundred whose hearts resemble the heart of Adam, forty whose hearts resemble the heart of Moses, seven whose hearts resemble the heart of Abraham, five whose hearts resemble the heart of Gabriel, three whose hearts resemble the heart of Michael, and one whose heart resembles the heart of Seraphiel (Isrāfīl). Whenever the one dies God replaces him with one of the three, whenever one of the three dies God replaces him with one of the five, whenever one of the five dies God replaces him with one of the seven, whenever one of the seven dies God replaces him with one of the forty, whenever one of the forty dies God replaces him with one of the three hundred and whenever one of the three hundred dies God replaces him with one of the common people. It is through them that God the Exalted relieves this community's afflictions." Imām al-Yāfi'ī (may God's mercy be upon him) then said: "The one who resembles the heart of Isrāfīl is the *Quṭb*, the *Ghawth*. His position and rank among saints is that of the point at the center of the circle; by him the good functioning of the world is sustained." According to al-Khidr (may God's peace be upon him) "Three hundred are the saints, seventy are the *Nujabā'*, forty are the *Awtād* (pillars) of the earth, ten are the *Nuqabā'*, seven are the '*Urafā'*, three are the chosen ones, and one is the *Ghawth*."

According to Shaykh 'Abdal-Qādir al-Jīlānī (may God's mercy be upon him) the *Abdāl* are seven. Shaykh Aḥmad al-Rifā'ī (may God's mercy be upon him) said that the *Awtād* were four. And Shaykh Ibn 'Arabī (may God's mercy be upon him) said that around the *Quṭb* were two men named the two Imāms, one on his right looking toward the invisible world (*Malakūt*) and the other on his left looking toward the visible world (*Mulk*); when the *Quṭb* dies he is replaced by the one on his left. He also said (may God's mercy be upon him) "There are men among the saints termed *Afrād*, who are not under the *Quṭb's* jurisdiction, he may even not be aware of them at all." That is possible, however, the statements of Shaykh 'Abdal-Qādir al-Jīlānī (may God's mercy be upon him) indicate that the *Afrād*, as well as other saints, are all, by the will of God, under the *Ghawth's* authority.[16]

The saints of God the Exalted are not confined to these numbers. It has been said that in the days of Shaykh 'Abdal-Qādir (may God's mercy be upon him) they numbered twelve thousand. "*God's warriors are known only to Him.*" [74:31]

As for the *Quṭb*, the *Ghawth*, there is one in each time. He is the all comprehending *Fard*, and is known among the People as the *Khalīfa* (vice-regent) and the Perfect Man. He is also given the titles of *Ṣāḥib al-Ṣiddīqiyya al-Kubrā* (Possessor of the Degree of Supreme Veracity) and *al-Wilāya al-'Uẓmā* (Greatest Sainthood). Some of his attributes and inner experiences were mentioned by *Sayyidī* 'Abdal-Qādir (may God's mercy be upon him), and these were quoted by al-Yāfi'ī in the last story of "*Kitāb al-Sālikīn*" (The Book of the Travelers) where they can be found.

Poleship (*Quṭbāniyya*) is Lordship (*Siyāda*); this is why the term *Quṭb* is used analogically for whoever possesses lordship over the men of a particular spiritual station (*maqām*) or state (*ḥāl*). There is thus a 'Pole of the People of Reliance' (*Quṭb al-mutawakkilīn*), 'Pole of the People of Contentment' (*Quṭb al-Rāḍīn*), and so on. The 'Possessor of the Degree of Supreme Veracity' is called *al-Quṭb al-Ghawth* to prevent any confusion arising from such analogical use of the term *Quṭb*.

This should be sufficient explanation on this matter. There are differences among the People (*al-Qawm*) in their descriptions of the titles and numbers of such men, but these prove, on scrutiny, to be no more than differences in terminology.

To elaborate further would require us to mention the inner states of the men of the "Circle of Sainthood" (*Dā'irat al-Wilāya*), their characteristics, the differences within each rank, and other such things, the knowledge of which belongs by right only to the *Quṭb*, the *Ghawth* who encompasses all their ranks and whose rank and state comprehend every single one of theirs. As for the other saints, they know about those who are of equal or lesser ranks. They are aware of those above them but have no full knowledge of them.

On the whole, these are questions which can be answered satisfactorily only by contemplation (*mushāhada*) and unveiling (*kashf*) and whoever desires this should discipline his soul, reduce its density with the kind of arduous effort that annihilates the soul's frivolity and conquers its passions, and embellish it with constant attentiveness to God the Exalted, courtesy, submissiveness, humility, powerlessness, and poverty in the realization of servitude (*'ubūdiyya*) and the fulfilling of the rights of Lordship (*Rubūbiyya*)[17]. Whenever a servant masters these two basic things, effective discipline and perfect presence, the veil over his heart is rent, then he beholds the 'Unseen of his Lord' and sees the saints, in their ranks and holy functions, as pure spirits. He then no longer needs descriptions and rises from the trough of having to follow others to the peak of contemplation. As for us who are veiled, we have to make do with mere descriptions, in this as in other similar matters. However, as long as one does not stop there, these will not be insignificant; for love is their result, and from it longing, then seeking, and he who seeks finds. "*News each have their appointed time.*" [6:67] "*And to each term its written decree.*" [13:38]

4

The illumined Shaykh, 'Abdal-Kabīr ibn 'Abdallāh Bā-Ḥumayd questioned him about the position of someone who mixes with sinful persons and eats of the food of people whose [commercial] transactions are unsound, how should one behave toward him?

He answered (may God be pleased with him): Know that no believer concerned for his religion and his life-to-come should associate with or keep the company of any but the people of goodness and conformity, those who fear God the Exalted and avoid sins whether by steering away from them altogether or by sound repentance if ever they do fall into one. As for the man who associates with [habitual sinners] but only as much as necessary and no more, who finds their sins repugnant, reproves them and urges them to repent, his faith is secure and no harm will come to him through his association with them. This behavior may even become recommended if there is hope that they will be influenced by his advice and accept his invitation [to turn back to God] even if after some time. As for the man who associates with them and does not reproach them for their sins while in a position to do so, but neither joins nor assists them in committing them, he is not free of blame and may well receive his share of anything that befalls them, especially if his associating with them had not been due to necessity. Lastly, the man who associates with sinners, praises them, approves of their caprices, and perhaps helps them to fulfill their depraved wishes, he is considered by God to be worse than they are and will be swifter to receive God's punishment and more deserving of His wrath. These considerations relate to those who are persistent sinners, openly display their sinful behavior and are well known by others to be committing them. On the whole, a sane man should avoid mixing with persistent sinners, unless they are brought together by a chance meeting, a social occasion, or attending a public place such as a mosque or a market. This is because associating with them hardens the heart, weakens one's determination in obedience, and drags one into sin by virtue of the influence that God the Exalted, in His wisdom, causes to be transmitted between people who like and associate with each other. Those who have experienced these things know about them.

As for dealing with and eating the food of someone whose transactions include some that are unsound: if most of his transactions are sound, and he possesses crops which are truly his, and the licit in his wealth exceeds the suspect and the illicit, then, as scholars have stated (may God have mercy on them), it is permissible to eat of his food and have dealings with him. Circumspection, however, should induce one to avoid such things as much as possible.

And God the Exalted knows best.

5

The same man questioned him about the remedy for one who is slow to acts of goodness, inclined to pleasures, but is fond of goodness and good people and finds evil and evil people repugnant.

He answered (may God be pleased with him and with his ancestors): Know that this state of affairs has four causes:

The first is ignorance and its remedy is the acquisition of knowledge.

The second is weakness of faith and it can be strengthened by reflecting on the dominion of the heavens and earth and persevering in good works.

The third is harboring long hopes. Its remedy is to remember death and be constantly aware that it may pounce on you at any moment.

The fourth is eating suspect food. The solution for this is to be circumspect and to consume little amounts even of that which is *ḥalāl*.

The one who remedies himself until he removes all these causes by doing their opposites in the manner that we have just mentioned, will become such that he will never tire of his acts of obedience nor ever get bored from any good thing. He would neither be attracted to nor find comfort in passionate desires and ephemeral pleasures. However, one should not expect this in his initial stages [on the path] for it is only achieved after much struggle; such is the pattern that God the Exalted has created, "*And you will find no changing in God's wont.*" [33:62] A man should first of all avoid all transgressions, wean himself from passionate desires and strive against inertia and the difficulties of persevering in obedience until he proves the sincerity of his approach to God, Transcendent and Exalted is He, and his desire to reform his heart and straighten his condition. God will then look at him and envelop him with His invisible solicitude. He will then find such delight and pleasure as cannot be exceeded in acts of obedience and goodness, and such extreme bitterness and aversion for passionate desires that for these simply to cross his mind would become unimaginable. That is God's favor which He bestows upon whom He will. He has said, Blessed and Exalted is He: "*Those who strive in Us We shall guide them on Our paths.*" [39:69] And: "*The gracious word of your Lord was fulfilled for the children of Israel because of what they patiently endured.*" [7:137] And "*God has promised those of you who have believed and done good that He shall give them sovereignty on earth.*" [14:55]

6–9

The same man also asked:

Is it better for the servant to conceal or openly display his activities?

Is fear better for him or hope?

Which of the Qur'ān, *tasbīḥ*, or *tahlīl* is better for a man wishing to have a *wird*?

Is it better to prolong one's standing (during the ritual prayer), inclinations, and prostrations, or to shorten them so as to be able to increase the number of supererogatory prayers?

He also asked his opinion concerning certain thoughts that came to him at night as well as at other times.

He also related to him that having heard a person speak of a horse and how it needed discipline and a teacher, he had applied these things to himself; and, how on another occasion, having heard someone speak of spring and the preparation and care that the land needed before and after the rainfalls, he had applied these things to his heart. He then asked him whether these manners of understanding were sound?

He also asked him about a dream, the details of which will become clear from the answer.

6

He answered him (may God increase him of His favors and give us of his *baraka*): Know that to display [one's devotions] is better for those who run no risk of becoming ostentatious and hope that some of their brothers will emulate them. But concealing them is better for those who do fear ostentation and do not expect anyone to emulate them. Concealing them is also better for those who, being safe from ostentation, nevertheless expect no one to follow them, and vice versa.

As for which is preferable, fear or hope, know that fear is preferable for those whose ego (*nafs*) is powerful and whose inclination toward sins is great, until such time as they become upright. Hope, on the other hand, is preferable for those on the verge of death, so that they may die thinking well of God the Exalted. As for those possessed of bodily health and firm adhesion to religion, it is better to have equal shares of fear and hope so that they may be as the two wings of a bird.

7

As for your question regarding which of the Qur'ān, *tahlīl* or *tasbīḥ*, would be more commendable for someone wishing to have a *wird*; know that nothing is better than reciting the Qur'ān with presence, reflection, and the appropriate intonation. However, boredom and weariness are part of human nature, one should therefore shift from one *wird* to another, recite [the Qur'ān] for a while, pray for a while, reflect about death and what follows it, then move on to other kinds of worshipping activities.

8

As for which is preferable, to prolong one's standing, inclinations and prostrations, or shorten them so as to increase the number of *rak'as* during supererogatory devotions; know that what has been handed down concerning the behavior of the Messenger of God (may blessings and peace be upon him) during his night vigils, is that he prolonged his standing, inclinations and prostrations to great lengths but did not exceed eleven or thirteen *rak'as*. Scholars (may God's mercy be on them) have differed regarding which was better, to prolong one's standing or one's inclinations and prostrations; some have advocated the first, others the second. Imām al-Ghazālī and others are of the opinion that that which brings on more awe and presence is preferable, and that this is bound to change with the changes in one's inner states.

9

As for the thoughts that you say come to you at night as well as at other times, know that reflection has a great share in the reformation and rectitude of the heart and in bringing to life good intentions and acts. Not every kind of thinking, of course, but reflection on the manifest signs of God the Exalted, the visible marvels of His creation, the multiplicity of His gifts and favors, that which He has promised to honor His friends with in the abode of reward and that which He has threatened to humiliate His foes with in the abode of punishment. Also included is reflection on the world's evanescence, chaotic conditions, multitude of troubles and [numerous] kinds of foulness. As for thinking of the passionate desires and pleasures toward which the ego is attracted, if it is from the point of view that they are upsetting, troubling, ephemeral and driven [by God] towards His foes and away from those He loves, this is profitable thinking. But if it is from the point of view of their being well suited to the ego, conforming to one's nature, comforting and pleasurable, to the extent of envying those who have access to them, as occurs with those whose hearts are unaware of their Lord, then this kind of thinking is not permissible; it is ugly and reprehensible since it stimulates desire and greed for worldly things, and the effort to acquire and accumulate them.

As for your hearing someone speak of a horse and its need for discipline and teaching, and your application of that to yourself and your need for one of the men of God to discipline and teach you good manners with his words and deeds, as well as that which you heard about spring and the land's need for preparation and care before and after the rainfalls, and your application of that to your heart and its need, when the rains of wisdom fall on it, for preparation and care from the shaykhs through their solicitude and discipline, all of that is "correct audition" (*samā' mustaqīm*) and enlightened understanding. The People (may God be pleased with them) call this kind of audition "free audition" (*samā' muṭlaq*) which means that whatever is heard is taken to apply to that in which one is currently engaged in his traveling along the path and his [effort to] conform to the Supreme Assembly (*al-mala' al-a'lā*), each according to his state and station. However, they stipulate, as a condition, that this happen suddenly and spontaneously without prior thinking of affectation. They have many stories to this effect, for example the one about three of them who once heard a man calling: "Wild Thyme!" (*Sa'tar barrī!*) at which they became ecstatic and lost awareness [of their physical environment]. When subsequently questioned about it the first replied: "I heard the Real addressing me thus: 'Strive and you shall see My beneficence!'" (*Is'a tara birrī!*) The second said: "I heard: 'How vast is My beneficence!'" (*Mā awsa'a birrī!*) And the third said: "I heard: 'Now you will see My beneficence!'" (*Al-sā'a tarā birrī!*) See, may God have mercy on you, how, from the Presence, they received such a majestic address!

As for that which you saw in your dream, that you were reading the *'Awārif* of Suhrawardī before a *sharīf* that you know does no such thing, this should be taken to mean that something good relating to this path, the path of the Sufis, will come to you from whence you expect it not.

And as for that writing which you saw in [the other] dream on the hand of a man not known for his rectitude and which included the mention of mercy and the name of Joseph, its interpretation is that mercy will come to that man and its manner will be either that people will accuse him of something he is innocent of, or that he will forgive someone who has injured him, or some other such thing similar to what happened to God's Prophet Joseph (may God's peace be upon him).[18] The important thing is that the dream be true and free from the enticements of the ego and the insinuations of the devil. At the very least the dreamer's tongue should be truthful in his waking state and his heart and head free from corrupt imaginations and from talking of things which are remote from the truth. The Messenger of God (may God's blessings and peace be upon him) said: "A Sound dream is one of forty-six parts of Prophethood."

A Conclusion on Repentance which was led up to by what has just been said: Know that repentance is that wide open door of God the Exalted and a grace of His, Transcendent is He, which He bestows on those who approach Him. It means that one is to refrain from everything that God wants him to refrain from, such as sins and prohibited things, and that one should find them repugnant; and that one is to engage in everything that God wants him to do and would dislike him to neglect, such as obligatory acts and duties.

The one who neglects any of his obligations or falls into doing something prohibited then wishes to repent should refrain from the prohibited act and perform the [neglected] duty; he should experience remorse for his shortcomings and resolve never to behave in such a manner again for the rest of his life. The one who repents and then repeats [his act] will not thereby invalidate his previous repentance, but he should repent again. This is part of the grace that God shows us and all other people, so let Him be praised, we shall never praise Him enough; He is as He has praised Himself.[19]

According to a *ḥadith*, God the Exalted extends His Hand at night so that those who did wrong during the day may repent and He extends His Hand during the day so that those who did wrong during the night may repent. And there is a gate in the West, as wide as the distance traveled by the sun in forty days, which remains open for repentance and is never shut until the day the sun rises from whence it [now] sets. And God, Transcendent and Exalted is He, accepts His servant's repentance as long as the latter is not gasping. Gasping means that he is dying, his spirit has reached his throat and he is in his last few breaths.

You are now aware of the rules of repentance and its status in religion. It remains to be said that anyone who has done another an injustice must return what he has appropriated if it is money, or surrender himself for legal retaliation or ask for pardon if [the offence was against] someone's life or honor. If this proves to be totally impossible, then he has to do whatever part of it he can. It is to be hoped that by God's grace his adversaries will forgive him in the life-to-come.

If he has neglected any of his obligations, such as ritual prayers, fasts or *zakāt*, the repentant must perform all that he has neglected; this cannot be avoided, but can be done at some leisure and as one's circumstances allow, with neither too much constraint nor too much indulgence, for this religion is resilient. The Prophet has said (may blessings and peace be upon him): "I was sent with the tolerant primordial pattern (*al-ḥanīfiyya*)." And: "Make it easy, do not make it difficult. Give good tidings and do not cause aversion."

It has reached us that one of our virtuous predecessors persisted for a long time in asking God the Exalted to grant him a sincere repentance (*tawba nasūḥ*) without perceiving any sign that he was being answered. He became perplexed until he saw in his dream that he was being told: "'*God does indeed love those who repeatedly repent and He loves those who purify themselves.*'" [2:222] May God grant us and you a sincere repentance, in a goodly state and in well being, and may He take us to Him in such a state!

10

The illumined Shaykh, Muḥammad ibn Aḥmad Sal'ān, questioned him about the utterance of the gnostic Shaykh, Abū-Yazīd al-Bisṭāmī (may God be pleased with him): "The farthest people from God the Exalted are those who refer to Him most frequently."

He replied: If the Shaykh - may God's mercy be on him- means the common people by the "farthest people," it would be because for them to frequently refer to God, Transcendent and Exalted is He, by saying, "This is for God," or any other similar thing, would indicate ostentation and imitating the elite to appear equal to them. Such people are undoubtedly farther away from God than the others. And if by "people" the Shaykh (may God's mercy be upon him) means the élite among gnostics, and this is a common usage of the word, then it would mean that the gnostic who frequently refers to God the Exalted is farther away from the Divine Presence than other gnostics, because reference can only be made at a distance and in the absence of contemplation.

11

He also questioned him about the saying: "The soul addressed the heart thus: 'Be with me in ordinary activities so that I can be with you in devotional activities.'"

He answered: This is the 'serene soul' addressing the enlightened heart. When the heart is present with it in its necessary ordinary activities such as eating, drinking and so on, the soul achieves rectitude in carrying out those activities, through this presence, always choosing the best alternative. And when the soul is present with the heart in devotional activities it supplies it with energy and is a sign that both the inward and the outward aspects have joined forces.

When the inward is with the outward in its activities and the outward with the inward in its transformation, they are in perfect unison for the achievement of [spiritual] goals.

12

> He also questioned him about whether the shaykh should be loved for himself, his qualities, or the comfort that he provides?

He answered: Know that to love [someone] for the excellence and beauty of his qualities is a love that is rational, and so is also to love him for the benefits obtained from him, whether these be worldly or religious. The first kind is the more noble and profitable.

To love someone for himself is conceivable only in the case of the Real, Eminent and Majestic is He. It is subtle and mysterious and poses a problem for other than the people of insight. There is absolutely nothing that should be loved for itself except God the Exalted.

As for it having been said about the members of the house of Prophethood whose behavior was mixed: "We detest their attributes but not their selves," this is because their physical selves descend from the Prophet. This is not the same as what we have just been saying.

13

> And he questioned him about the prayer of the Prophet (may blessings and peace be upon him) for Ibn 'Abbās: "O God, grant him the understanding of religion and teach him interpretation."

He answered: To understand religion is to understand its sciences and inquire into the wisdom and secrets [within them], so that the practice of religion becomes based on understanding and insight. As for the science of interpretation it is the interpretation of the Qur'ān and *Sunna*. Ibn 'Abbās (may God be pleased with him) was the ultimate in that field, he was called the "Interpreter of the Qur'ān" and this was because of the Messenger of God's prayer for him. We may use the same prayer and we may add to it: "And guide us to the even path," which is the way to the good pleasure of God the Exalted and to His Garden, in a manner that is easy and wholesome. So let all who utter this prayer mean by it that which we have just mentioned, that is, the understanding of religion, the science of interpretation, and guidance to [and along] the path. Then, when God the Exalted answers them, they will be granted that which is most suitable and profitable to them and had been decreed for them.

14

> And he questioned him about his saying (may God's blessings and peace be upon him) that God the Exalted says: "Those who are too occupied with the remembrance of Me…"[20]

He answered: It appears to me that it refers to the ones whose state is to be absorbed in the remembrance, dissolved in it, losing all restraint, and making it their [sole] occupation and habit. When such people do not pray (*du'ā'*) much during this period, they miss nothing of that which those who pray abundantly receive.

On the contrary, they receive more than those who ask since they are occupied with God the Exalted and His remembrance and not with others or with their own share [of the world].

I see no justification for a person who is praying to abandon his prayers (*du'ā'*) for invocation (*dhikr*).

I do not believe this to be good, and cannot say that this is the intention behind the *ḥadith*, for prayers (*du'ā'*) are also invocations and in them are neediness for God the Exalted and awe and humility toward Him that are lacking in other devotions. This is why it was said that: "Prayer (*du'ā'*) is the marrow of worship."[21]

15

> Shaykh 'Abdallāh Bā-Sa'īd al-'Amūdī questioned him about the utterance of the great Shaykh Sa'īd ibn 'Īsā (may God be pleased with him): "A shaykh is not a shaykh until he knows the principles (*uṣūl*) of religion and their applications (*furū'*)." After which he added: "The principles are seven and the applications seventy."

He answered: Know that this statement of the shaykh is true and authoritative. As for his saying: "until he knows the principles of religion and their applications," it means that the shaykh who summons [others to God] must possess the knowledge of the principles and the applications of religion either in sum or in detail, either by acquisition and learning or by way of grace and inspiration. The latter was indeed the case of Shaykh Sa'īd, for he was illiterate, as were a number of other shaykhs such as Shaykh Aḥmad al-Ṣayyād, 'Alī al-Ahdal, Abul-Ghayth, and others (may God have mercy on them all).

As for the shaykh's statement that the principles are seven and the applications seventy, it cannot be analyzed with any accuracy, for the shaykh may have had in mind some inner meanings which would constitute principles and applications in the manner stated. As someone once said: "A shaykh must have firmly established the practice of obligations and supererogations." Then added: "The obligation is to love the Lord and the supererogation is to renounce the world."

The gist of what the shaykh said is that a shaykh must possess religious knowledge, both inward and outward, to perfection. It has been said: "God never took an ignorant man unto Himself[22], for when He takes him He teaches him."

16

The same shaykh also asked him about the saints of the circles, their numbers and other things which will appear from the answer.

He answered: Some of these things were mentioned by the Shaykh the Imām 'Abdallāh ibn As'ad al-Yāfi'ī at the beginning of "*Rawḍ al-Rayāḥīn*", so look them up there. We have been asked about this matter and have given an answer in one of our treatises.

As for the first ever to be established in the degree of Poleship (*Quṭbaniyya*), it has been said that it was al-Ḥasan son of 'Alī (may God be pleased with them). It has also been said that it was Abū-Bakr (may God be pleased with him), then the Caliphs in the order they came, then al-Ḥasan, al-Ḥusayn and Zayn al-'Ābidīn. This is what has been said. As for the last to be established in it, it is the Mahdī, may peace be upon him, the Fāṭimī, whose coming is at the end of time.

The Pole is the best among the faithful of the time. The rest of what you inquire about is mentioned in "*Rawḍ al-Rayaḥīn*" in a general way. To detail such a matter requires much elaboration and some of that knowledge is of the kind that it is not permissible to put into books.

17

And he asked him about a certain person's statement that the denial of the *karāmāt* of the saints amounted to disbelief (*kufr*), when most scholars have already decided that it is to be considered an innovation (*bid'a*).

He answered: We go by what the scholars have said concerning this matter. The statement quoted in "*Laṭā'if al-*

Minan"[23] and attributed to Shaykh Abū-Turāb al-Nakhshabī (may God have mercy on him) is to be interpreted as meaning a kind of disbelief short of [total] disbelief, or to apply to those who deny the possibility of their occurrence as a matter of Divine Ability or from any other point of view.

As for *karāmāt* being the same as *mu'jizāt*, this is only by virtue of their being secondary to them, not in themselves; they are not the same and are in most respects dissimilar. A *mu'jiza* is a proof of the Messenger's veracity whereas a *karāma* from a saint who firmly upholds the Law, is a proof of the excellence of his following his Prophet and of the truth of his religion. This is why it is said that each saint's *karāma* is but a *mu'jiza* of the Prophet whom he follows. Great is the difference between a *karāma* and a *mu'jiza*, so do understand!

18

He also asked about the interrogation of people in their graves; do both [angels] carry out the interrogation or only one? In which language is it done? Are they two or three? Do they metamorphose and change form according to the dead person's state?

He answered: As for the two angels' interrogation it is true, real and beyond doubt. Everything else is unnecessary once there is certainty concerning the reality of the interrogation. There are a few weak *ḥadiths* relating to your questions, but the important thing is simply to believe in the two angels' interrogation. The traditionist, al-Suyūṭī (may God have mercy on him), quotes in his book "*Sharḥ al-Ṣudūr fī Aḥwāl Ahl al-Qubūr*"[24] what should be sufficient concerning this matter and you may read it if you wish.

19

Al-'Amūdī also asked him: Is the Garden in the heavens and the fire in the seventh earth? In which state will the earth and the heavens be on the Day of Rising, will they be altered or will God create different ones? How many degrees are there in the Garden and how many Gardens? What is it that enables the believers to see God, Majestic and High is He, in the hereafter?

He answered: Know, may God grant you success and make you of those whose inner eye is enlightened and perceives by the light of God the Exalted, that this knowledge was handed down both in sum and in detail. However, even when detailed, much remains implicit, for human minds are incapable of bearing it otherwise. It is enough for a man to have faith with certainty according to the text of the Book and *Sunna*.

As for the Garden, the apparent meaning of the Qur'ān is that it is in heaven and is of many degrees, one hundred in some versions, while others state that they are as many as the verses in the Qur'ān, which exceed six thousand.

There are eight Gardens and each contains many gardens. The uppermost is the Highest *Firdaws* and it has as its roof the Throne of the Merciful, Blessed and Exalted is He!

The inhabitants of the Garden are the Prophets and Messengers, and the good among the believers and the Muslims. Their degrees therein vary according to their faith and their deeds, some are finer than others and some are higher than others, but none are low or base.

As for the strength to see God the Exalted in the Garden, He will give them of His own strength and will fashion them at the resurrection in a way capable of sustaining it. These will be spirits and bodies to subsist, not liable to suffer from weaknesses or undergo the changes which ephemeral things are subjected to. In this manner will they be strong enough.

As for the earth and heavens on the Day of Rising, it is understood that they will change and metamorphose, both being included in God's decree of annihilation of both the physical and subtle worlds. This is indicated by His saying, Exalted is He: "*The day when the earth shall be changed and the heavens.*" [14:48] and: "*When heaven is rent asunder.*" [84:1] They will then be recreated as the previous heaven and earth but having been annihilated and changed from one state into another, as will also happen to the children of Adam and the other creatures. This is what can be understood and God knows best what the truth of the matter is.

As for the Fire, may God protect us all from it, it was said that it was now under the seventh earth and also that it was under the seas. It consists of tiers which number seven. The uppermost is *Jahannam*; it is for the sinners among the people of Unification. The lowermost is *al-Hāwiya*, that which has no bottom and no fathomable depth.

On the Day of Rising the Sovereign Requiter will appear and judge His creatures. The Throne of the Merciful will be brought forth, then the Garden will be brought forth to its right and the Fire to its left, then every creature shall be summoned for the final judgment. Some will end up in the Garden and some in the Fire. "*Judgment shall be given according to the Truth and it shall be said: Praise to God, Lord of the Worlds.*" [39:75]

There is in the Book and the *Sunna* much detail on the subject, so search and meditate on it and take a firm hold of the summary which we have given you, for it contains the essence of what is required. The one who believes in God is rightly-guided.

20

I questioned him about 'preferring others to oneself', does it include both the things of this world and those of the next or is it confined to worldly matters involving the soul's wishes and desires?

He answered: Know that to prefer others to oneself in worldly matters and passions is a great virtue. This was the wont of our virtuous predecessors and those who emulated and succeeded them. Many interesting stories to that effect exist and some of these are mentioned by Imām al-Ghazālī in the chapter on "Deprecating Wealth" in the *"Iḥyā'"* as was also done by others.

As for preferring others to oneself in other-worldly matters such as religious practices, we know of no worthwhile opinions to that effect. For this would indicate a lack of desire to draw nearer to God the Exalted and attain to His good pleasure and these are things which one should hasten to and compete and jostle for.

There are a few stories of people affiliated to Sufism and in spiritual states (*ḥāl*) which seem to indicate something of the kind, however, a spiritual state should be conceded to its man, provided it is sincere, but not emulated.

There are also certain kinds of devotions which are perilous, some people are more suited to these than others, some hold back in view of the dangers involved and leave them to others who are more able to perform them. Examples of such activities are leading the ritual prayers, leading a nation, giving legal opinions, teaching religious sciences, and so on. But if you observe carefully the states of those who give precedence to others in such matters you will find that the reason behind it is still their attempt to seek the proximity of God the Exalted and avoid His wrath, which they may become exposed to should they expose themselves to these dangers or to any other thing which may threaten their religion.

21

I also asked him about the times for the morning and evening invocations.

He answered: As for morning and evening, they say that evening begins when the sun is at its zenith and morning after midnight or the last third of the night. And as for the invocations specific to these times, the evening ones are better recited when night is near, as for instance the time when [the sun] turns yellow, and at the beginning of the night; and the morning ones from before dawn until sunrise. This is the way in which we ourselves perform this noble *wird*.

22

And I asked him about "rubbing [one's body] after reciting [certain protective verses of the Qur'ān] and blowing into one's palms at bedtime", as the Prophet (may blessings and peace be upon him) is reported to have done; should one rub the whole body even at the cost of some discomfort? For the *ḥadith* says: "That which he is able [to reach] of his body."

He answered: If a man recites and blows into his palms then passes his hands over his body of it, he should therefore rub those parts he is able to reach beginning with his head and face, then the front of his body.

23

And I asked him about the meaning of 'traveling' to God the Exalted.

He answered: Know that traveling (*sulūk*) with both the body and the heart is by purifying the soul and the senses from reprehensible attributes and behavior, then adorning them with excellent attributes and behavior. This is how the servant draws nearer to the Presence of God the Exalted, and this nearness is that of the heart. The purer and better he becomes, the closer he will draw.

There is another kind of traveling to God the Exalted which is subtler and finer but unsuitable to be mentioned except to those who are done or nearly so with the first kind.

24

And I asked him about the statement of certain people of the path that one should not talk about spiritual states and stations if one has yet to reach them.

He answered: This is so and it applies more particularly to the disciple (*murīd*) who is traveling the path but is yet to realize those states and stations; his talking or inquiring about them may result in a certain amount of affectation, self-admiration, ostentation, or other similar things which hinder and confuse the traveler. Therefore, they will only permit him to inquire about the stations and states he is actually going through if they cause him confusion. He is then permitted to consult his shaykh if this is possible, if not then any other man of the path, or if it so happens that none is at hand, their books. These are the general rules concerning this matter.

25

And I asked him, what should one do who is standing before God, Majestic and High is He, either in prayer or in a similar situation, and fears that were he to allow himself to be [fully] aware of the Divine Presence he would either experience such awe that his prayer would be disrupted or, should thoughts of limitation or anthropomorphism occur to him in that Presence, be guilty of discourtesy?

He answered: The one who is anxious about the first situation should allow into his awareness only as much as his heart is able to sustain, after which if he does lose control he will be excused. As for the second situation, he should make himself aware that God sees [his outward], surrounds him [wherever he is] and knows [his inward], and he should never think or try to feel that he sees God, Transcendent and Exalted is He. One would thus be safe from imagining that God has a form or bears any resemblance to anything. This applies to those whose knowledge of God's Majesty and Holiness is feeble, the knowledge meant here being that of direct experience and contemplation, not that of belief and reflection.

26

And I asked him about the blameworthy desire of the disciple for *karāmāt* and unveilings in the manner mentioned in the "Treatise of the Disciple".

He answered: This is blameworthy because it may lead to one's zeal and perseverance in worship becoming solely for that purpose; one would thus join the company of those who are pursuing worldly things and passions. This applies to those who seek outward *karāmāt*, such as the folding up of distances, speaking of hidden things, and so on. As for those who seek true *karāmāt* such as increased faith and certitude, the realization of the relinquishment of all desire for the world, the aspiration for the hereafter and other such things, these are praiseworthy for they are part of religion and the truth which should be aspired for and pursued.

27

And I asked him about the statement of Imām al-Ghazālī in the chapter on thankfulness in the *"Iḥyā"* that the Angels of Proximity are more thankful to God the Exalted than the Prophets, and about other similar statements implying that the angels are superior to the Prophets.

He answered: Know that this is the opinion of some of the *Ahl al-Sunna* and it has been said that Imām al-Ghazālī was one of them; but the majority hold a different opinion.

I say: The words of Ghazālī (may God's mercy be on him) in this and other similar passages express the opinion that they are indeed superior but only in certain respects, and with this I concur. I cannot allow myself to speak of this for it belongs to the Divinc Mysteries. The opinion to be trusted is that of the majority of *Ahl al-Sunna*, which is also the opinion of Imām al-Ghazālī, as can be seen from other relevant passages.

28

And I asked him about the use of invocations and prayers containing non-Arabic words by those who do not know their meaning and about using the invocation *Yā-Hū*! *Yā-Hū*!

He answered: We have already mentioned verbally to you that when these things are found in the prayers of those who are both authoritative scholars as well as gnostics and who join knowledge to certitude, such as Imām al-Ghazālī, Shaykh al-Suhrawardī, Shaykh Abul-Ḥasan al-Shādhilī, and their like (may God be pleased with them all and spread their benefit), there is no harm for the invoker and the supplicant to use them; they would thus be following those who are worthy to be [trusted and] followed. On the other hand, if such words are used by those who do not fit this description, one should refrain from using them until their meaning becomes known, for they may contain meanings which belong to disbelief or border on it.

As for remembrance using *Yā-Hū*, it should be confined to those whose state is total absorption, as stated by Shaykh

Zarrūq (may God's mercy be on him) unless one comes across them in the litanies (*aḥzāb*) of the people of realization, in which case one would be following them and not subject to presumptuousness or innovation.

29

> And I asked him about the meaning of the words of the *Quṭb, sayyid* Abū-Bakr son of the supreme *Ghawth, sayyid* 'Abdallah ibn Abū-Bakr al-'Aydarūs 'Alawī (may God be pleased with them): "The lover is drunk, yet in him there is no drunkenness," up to the verse that says: "God does what He wills, whether of possible or impossible things."

He answered: It seems that your perplexity arises from his saying, "or impossible," seeing that it has been agreed among theologians that the impossible is that which cannot be conceived to exist. The meaning that appears to us in the words of the Shaykh is that should the Divine Will be aimed at an impossibility it would bring it into existence and the irresistible Ability would not be powerless before it. However, Divine Will never aims at impossibility. The Shaykh (may God's mercy be on him) made this clear when he said: "God does what He wills." When He wills He does, but He never wills impossibility therefore it can never be. In the same vein should one understand the verse that states: "*Had God wished to take a son unto himself He would have.*" [39:4]. A son is impossible for Him, therefore He never wills it. There is another possible meaning for the Shaykh's words which is that he means here by the 'impossible' those things which are possible but thought to be extremely unlikely. It is sometimes done in the Arabic language to call such things impossible; unlikely things are described by people thus: "This is impossible and that is impossible." Such use of the word is acceptable among Arabs and in line with other metaphorical expressions. There is a third meaning to the Shaykh's words but it cannot be divulged except by Divine permission and then only to those worthy of it, for it requires subtle understanding and most minds would fail to grasp it. This is what we have understood from the Shaykh's words, may God spread his benefit!

30

> And I asked him about the meaning of the utterance of our master the Imām 'Alī ibn Abī Ṭālib (may God honor his face and allow us to benefit from his *baraka)*: "Give life to your devotional gatherings by sitting with those before whom one is shy."

He answered: It seems that the problem here lies in taking shyness to mean ostentation. When the motive behind an act of obedience is concern for what other people think, then it would be to a certain extent ostentatious. However, ostentation has nothing to do with shyness. The first is to act in obedience for the sake of the rank and status to be attained with people and in the pursuit of profit, whether it is wealth or prestige. The second is a certain constriction that a man of noble character experiences in those situations that produce it and which drives him towards acts of goodness and the avoidance of base behavior. It is often experienced in the company of the virtuous. There is a *ḥadith* that says: "Be shy before God as you would be before a man of virtue." And ibn Sīrīn (may God be pleased with him) spoke about the opposite kind of situation thus: "I see that the whole of wickedness lies in keeping the company of those whose presence does not impose shyness." It has also reached us that Anas ibn Mālik (may God be pleased with him) was once asked why he had concealed himself from those he saw coming out of the Friday prayer which he had missed, he said: "Those are shameless with God who are shameless with people." He may have attributed these words to the Messenger of God (may God's blessings and peace be upon him) but, being in some doubt, I have refrained from stating it to be so, for it is perilous to speak falsely about the Messenger of God (may God's blessings and peace be upon him) and severe threats were proffered against those who do so.

31

> And I asked him whether a young boy, guilty of ostentation, loses his reward; what should one think of such behavior?

He answered: Know that a boy, until he reaches puberty, is one of those against whom the 'pen' records nothing. Therefore, his acts of hypocrisy are not sins. However, when his hypocrisy involves acts of obedience or devotions his reward is lost, whereas when sincere he does receive it. It is said that the rewards for a boy's actions are recorded in his parents' leaves. It would not be too far to say that the evil in the boy's hypocrisy reflects on those whose duty it is to guide him and teach him sincerity, whether these be his parents, custodians or any other person of similar function. These should exhort children to perform their duties such as prayers and fasts and prevent them from transgressions such as adultery and drinking.

32

> Shaykh 'Abdallāh ibn Aḥmad al-Zubaydī asked him about those whose intention in acting is to obtain the rewards for their act in the hereafter.

He answered: This is a praiseworthy motive and a blessed effort which will be well rewarded and it is what the virtuous believers have done, both the ancients and the latecomers. The servant is created weak and poor; he cannot do without the favors of his Rich Great Lord. This is the answer in short, one can elaborate on it at great length, but here is a brief explanation: those who work for the sake of God the Exalted can be divided into three kinds:

Those who work because they fear punishment and these are the 'fearful'.
Those who work because they are desirous of the reward and these are the 'hopeful'.
Finally those who work simply to conform to the [Divine] orders and these are the 'gnostics'.

The 'gnostics' cannot dispense with hope and fear, nor the 'fearful' with hope and knowledge, but the designation of each servant depends on his dominant station and state. Some Sufis have implied that the states of those who work in the hope of reward and the fear of punishment are deficient or low and this should be taken to mean that one should be aware that those who work simply to conform to orders are superior to those who have hopes and fears. This is indeed so, but these are degrees, some higher than others, and it is not the servant's (i.e. not within his ability) to establish himself in the one of his choice, for the matter belongs to God the Exalted, He is the One Who establishes those of His servants whom He will in whichever location He will. And the Real inevitably establishes in each of the three degrees a group of believers whose states become good and whose hearts become sound only by working according to the degree they are established in.

Some people of gnosis, when deprecating the degree of those who work in hope and fear, refer in reality to those who would have not worked at all had they had no wish for reward nor fear of punishment, whose hearts contain neither the respect nor awe for the Real that should lead them to conform to His commands and prohibitions. The matter is somewhat obscure and I have seen things attributed to certain people of the path which appear wrong or extravagant. I say: to work to obey orders and seek the good pleasure and proximity [of God] is laudable and good. To work in the hope of reward and awe of punishment is also laudable and good. Only the all-embracing among the people of God work according to all three degrees in a full and perfect manner, but this is rare. Let each man know where he stands and act accordingly. Be not like the bad hired-hand who works only when given his wage, nor like the bad slave who shows courtesy only when afraid of being beaten. Work for the sake of God the Exalted, because He is the Lord and Master and has ordered some things done and others avoided. Hope for your reward and attribute it to God's generosity and benevolence. Fear the punishment deserved by your lack of courtesy and shortcomings in worshipping your Lord and hope to be accorded safety from it by way of God's pardon and graciousness. This is the flexible pattern, the white road. Thus did behave the virtuous and the scholars. Any man possessed of insight who reflects on their words and behavior will understand what we have just said, take it with certainty, ask God for forgiveness and praise Him abundantly.

33

He also asked him which was better, to remember God silently or aloud?

He answered: Know that the gnostic scholars have said much about this. The gist of it is that silent remembrance is better when one fears being ostentatious, disturbing another who is praying, or any other such thing. When no such danger exists then uttering it aloud is better because it involves more effort, its benefit spreads to others and it has a stronger effect on one's presence and concentration. This, however, is for the feeble hearted whose presence is imperfect and absorption [in God] incomplete. There is a *ḥadith* to the effect that the best remembrance is the hidden one. And the Qur'ān says: "*Remember your Lord in yourself.*" [7:205] There are other *ḥadiths* mentioning [remembrance] done aloud. There is, therefore, good in both, the differences being due to the variability of persons and circumstances. Let the invoker do what he feels is better for his heart, more collecting for his determination, and more suitable for his state. And God knows best.

34

> Shaykh al-Zubaydī also asked him about the saying of the Prophet (may God's blessings and peace be upon him): "There is a valley in Hell against which Hell itself cries out seventy times a day for protection; it has been prepared by God the Exalted for those scholars of this community who are hypocrites."

He answered: If he means (may God's blessings and peace be upon him) by the hypocrites of this community, those who outwardly display faith and obedience while they remain, in their hearts, totally lacking in them, and who behave thus out of ostentation, in order to acquire a certain reputation and keep their real natures hidden, then these are the attributes of the hypocrites who are devoid of faith and will abide forever in the fire. For them to be in that valley against which Hell itself cries out for protection means that their torment and punishment will be magnified on account of their fraudulent simulation and deceitfulness. But if he means by hypocrite scholars those who harbor faith but are so overcome by their love for social eminence and high status that they ostentatiously display their devotion and knowledge to achieve them, then their imprisonment in that valley can be interpreted in one of two ways: either the end of their lives will be sinister[25], may God the Exalted protect us, they will thus remain in perpetual torment and be in a state similar to those mentioned before, or they will be treated with harshness and severity by being cast into that valley, then they will be rescued and leave it by the mercy of God, in accordance with the immutable law that none whose heart contains the least amount of faith will be held in the fire perpetually. Hypocrisy is one of the greatest major sins, it is also the smaller kind of idolatry.

35

He also asked him about the reason why a certain man remembers [God] in abundance yet experiences none of the experiences of remembrance which belong to those who are able to taste them?

He answered: The reason is that his heart is unsound, being neither free from reprehensible attributes nor filled with praiseworthy ones. He fails to expel the thoughts and insinuations his soul entertains during remembrance, he has not severed the outward attachments which distract him from devoting himself fully to the remembrance of God the Exalted, he is not being disciplined by a shaykh possessed of the gnosis of God the Exalted and of the [knowledge of the] inward and the outward, and there are other reasons.

Those who, like us, have failed to fulfill those conditions must remember God the Exalted abundantly with their tongues and strive to achieve presence of the heart; this is how they are to expose themselves to the grants of God the Exalted and it is not unlikely that He will grant them relief from whence they do not expect it. They should not wonder that they do not experience any of the spiritual experiences that the people of the path find in remembrance, since the conditions leading to them remain unfulfilled.

36

And he asked him about a man who, as was described by some, experienced the invocation of the tongue together with the heart, then that of the heart while the tongue was silenced, then the heart also lost its ability to invoke but the meaning remained and flowed through his inward and outward parts. This third state, in which both the tongue and the heart are unable to invoke, he found most estranging.

He answered: This man should be regarded as subject to the spiritual experiences peculiar to the invokers and that state which he found estranging is in reality the noblest and highest ranking of the three. He has but one further fourth state of remembrance to achieve, which is the kernel of kernels and which is to contemplate the invoked and become lost in Him to himself and all other creatures, and even to his own extinction. This is the ultimate aim and the highest station. This man is in possession of much good, he is advancing on the path of those who remember God and have similar experiences.

May God the Exalted grant us and you the realization of the truths of certitude and elevate us to the station of excellence (*Iḥsān*) in the wake of our realization of the two stations of submission (*Islām*) and faith (*Īmān*).

37

And he also asked him about the state of absence which occurs to the invokers.

He answered: This is to be unaware of all but God the Exalted, even of one's own self and one's invocation, having become lost in the contemplation of the Invoked, Exalted is He. Such an absence is the ultimate presence, its occurrence is rare and its persistence rarer still.

38

He also asked him about those sicknesses of the heart for which no cause is known.

He answered: When the nature of the sickness is known [the cause is also known], for gnostics when they recognize the sickness know the cause. When the nature of the sickness is unknown then the heart should be treated with the general remedies that are effective for all its sicknesses. Such are, for example, the thoughtful recitation of the Qur'ān, perseverance in the remembrance of God the Exalted with attentiveness, the frequent remembering of death, keeping the company of the virtuous, reading useful books such as those of Ghazālī, and so on.

39

> And he asked him about a man whose good works bore him fruits in this world such as sweetness in communing with God the Exalted, and because of these he became even more eager for such works, would this flaw the perfection of his deeds?

He answered: Yes, this is a flaw that people should be wary of. They should not act for this purpose, nor be deceived by it, nor trust in it, for it may be a lure. They should thank God for what He has granted them and concentrate solely on Him to the exclusion of all else, whatever it may be.

40

> He also asked him which of these two persons was better: a man who remembers his sins and is so aggrieved that he wishes to die in this state for fear of falling into further sins or in awareness of the goodness of such a state, or one in the same situation who wishes death to be delayed so that he may be able to repent and reform his heart?

He answered: Both states are good and superior. The one in which a man is maintained most of the time is the one that is preferable and more suitable for him.

A situation was reported to us which, although not identical with yours, is nevertheless related. Three of our virtuous predecessors once met and one of them said: "I wish to die for I fear the effect of temptations on my religion." The second said: "I wish to live for I hope I shall be granted repentance or good works." And the third one said: "I neither wish to die nor to live, I wish only that which God the Exalted wishes and chooses [for me]." His words were met with admiration and approval by the others. All three states are good and superior and each of them was maintained on his own. The possessor of the third state is the most perfect because of his ready acceptance of God's choice. These are matters to be experienced and, since they can be grasped neither by an effort of the will nor by wishful thinking, it is not man's to choose that which suits and pleases him best.

41

> And he asked him whether the beginning of the quest (*irāda*) was a matter of choice and effort or of being overpowered and forced into it?

He answered: Disciples and travelers differ in this and can be divided into two groups: the first are travelers by choice and the expenditure of effort; they set out before being pulled (*jadhb*). The second are overpowered and forced into traveling; they are pulled (*majdhūb*) before they choose to travel. Some among the people of the path are of the opinion that those who tread the path before being pulled are superior and others that those who are pulled first then begin to travel are superior.

42

> And he asked him about a certain heat that some invokers experience inwardly when they concentrate, which then spreads outwardly to their limbs, then is followed by lassitude.

He answered: This heat is one of the things that come upon the invoker and consumes the blemishes that still remain in both the servant's inward and his outward. It is good and beneficial. However, if the invoker is anxious that he may be overcome by it then let him abandon the particular invocation he is engaged in and substitute for it prayers on the Messenger of God (may blessings and peace be upon him) and *lā ḥawla wa lā quwwata illā bil'llāh* (There is neither ability nor strength save from God.)

43

> He also asked him why the benefits consequent upon saying *lā ilāha illa'llāh* were said by the Messenger (may blessings and peace be upon him) to depend on certain conditions such as truthfulness and sincerity when it is well known that a Muslim does, in effect, utter it with truth and sincerity.

He answered: The matter is so, but the meaning of truth and sincerity in this context is explained in one *ḥadith* as that which keeps the utterer from sins and in another *ḥadith* that a man should never prefer this world to the next. It is as if what is meant by truth and sincerity here is the reality [of the testimony] and its goal. Both are sound only in those whose certitude is perfect and whose faith profound and sincere.

A believer should hope strongly [for God's mercy], fear strongly [his retaliation] and be pure from the soiling of illusion.

As for the *ḥadith* concerning the man with the records and the parchment, the testimony on the parchment card is one that has been accepted, although a Muslim must have uttered it numerous times. It has been said regarding His saying, Exalted is He: "*Whoso brings [to Judgment Day] a good deed receives ten the like of it.*" [6:160] That the condition for that is to bring it, not just do it, for one may do it but not bring it because it was not done as prescribed and was thus not received with acceptance and satisfaction.

Fear and hope must therefore remain, for they are the two remedies each of which corrects the other when it becomes excessive.

Sharī'a contains both the general and specific. It is a general source for a multitude of people, each taking from it according to his caliber and state and in this they are of many different degrees; each is intended with [specific] things. To go into the details of this would be too lengthy. "*Each people know their drinking place.*" [2:60] "*Eat and drink of God's providing.*" [2:60] "*And give thanks to God if it be Him indeed that you worship.*" [2:172].

44

He also inquired, among other things, about isolation (*'uzla*) and its rules.

He answered: You inquired about isolation and its rules in these corrupt upside-down times where people are mostly distracted and forgetful of working for their life to come, yet keen on this world, greatly preoccupied with it, eager to amass [its riches], and deceived by its ornamentation. And you said that to keep their company and mix with them had become perilous for that reason and because most of their conversation was slanderous, irrelevant and meaningless. It is as you say. Ability and power are only by God the Exalted, the Formidable! (*Wa lā ḥawla wa lā quwwata illā bil'llāhi al-'Aliyyi l 'Aẓīm!)* A man who is concerned for his religion should not keep the company of such people or frequent them of his own accord, otherwise he will suffer diminution and loss. If they are imposed on him by force of circumstances he must remain silent and refrain from joining in their conversation. He must counsel them gently whenever possible and draw their attention to the things which might reform and save them.

I can think of no excuse for someone to abandon the Friday and other congregational prayers under the pretext that the times are corrupt; neither can he forsake his obligation to preserve his kinship bonds by visiting his relatives from time to time. But it is my opinion that he should mix with the people of these times only as much as is necessary to fulfill his religious as well as his worldly needs. He must remain silent whenever they converse about what they should not and be of good counsel whenever he can. If they behave in a good and correct manner he should assist and join them. This is how a man of virtue living among Muslims should behave. The only other alternative is to avoid them and take to the deserts and other desolate places in order to preserve one's religion and give priority to the soundness of one's heart. These matters were explained in full by our master and leader the Proof of Islam al-Ghazālī, may God have mercy on him and grant us to benefit from him, in his "*Minhāj*" and he devoted a full volume of the "*Iḥyā'*" to them.

45

He also asked him whether the one who loves certain people but does not behave as they do will be with them unconditionally as can be understood from the *ḥadith*: "A man is with whom he loves."

He answered: It appears to us from the statements of authoritative commentators on this *ḥadith* that this is limited to some aspects of the matter and not to all of them. The one who loves must conform to the loved one in all things including Unification, the careful performance of obligatory acts, the avoidance of perilous prohibited acts, and the performance of whatever good works are within reach. For to love someone is to emulate and follow him as much as possible, no love is true otherwise, for it will then be nothing but words devoid of any reality. Al-Ḥasan al-Baṣrī (may

God have mercy on him) said: "Do not be deceived by the *ḥadith* 'A man is with whom he loves when [you suffer from] distraction, illusion and the desertion of good works, for the Jews and the Christians love their Prophets but are of a certainty not with them." Similarly, some of the heretics of this community love some of the Companions (may God's pleasure be on them) greatly, they are loyal to them and may go so far as to lose their lives for them; nevertheless, they are of a certainty not with them since they have gone against their way and example by detesting and disowning the other Companions for whom they show no loyalty, as well as by other innovations in religion. This matter is one on which there is no disagreement. As this is so with innovations, the same, or nearly so, will of necessity apply to transgressions, mixing [good with evil works] and persistent sinning. These are degrees of good and evil and [other degrees] can be measured in a similar manner.

The ugliest of ugly things is disbelief in all its many degrees; then innovations, which are not all equal; then depravity; then mixing [good with evil]; and these last two also exhibit many degrees. The opposite of all this can equally well be stated about good; so understand our indications and ponder on our words for they are both highly valuable and indispensable. With reflection the intended goal will appear and the meaning will become clear. God guides whom He will to a straight path.

46

He also asked other questions, but the letter was lost. However, the reply included the following: I think that this letter contained questions concerning certain conditions in which God the Exalted, through His preordaining and excellent arrangement, establishes some of His servants, and which of these conditions is superior to the others.

Know that for those who are established by God [Transcendent is He] in any condition that is legally unobjectionable such as poverty or affluence, eminence or obscurity, or other similar states, superiority lies in fulfilling the rights of God [Transcendent is He] that are necessary to that condition and in maintaining its required courtesies, than in desiring a condition different from the one they are established in, for they would thus be discourteous towards their Lord, the High and Majestic.

As for the man who inquires about [spiritual] stations to know which of them is better, without being himself established in any of them, it would be extremely lengthy to speak to him [about them]. However, for example, were he to ask which of anonymity or fame is superior, we would say: it will differ with different people; anonymity is better for those with certain attributes, while fame is better for those with different ones, for they then would be better than those in obscurity and vice versa. However, there is a difference between these two conditions, so reflect on it.

Moreover, the obscure cannot render themselves famous, neither can the famous render themselves obscure. This leaves only that which we have said, that is to observe where God the Exalted has established you and maintain the necessary courtesy towards Him as it should be.

47

He also inquired about some of the states of the soul (*nafs*) and about remembrance.

The reply included the following: ...and they mention in it the states of distraction, heedlessness, excess, illusion and forgetfulness of death and of [the need to] gather provision for the Appointed Time that are habitual to the souls of people who nevertheless believe in God, His Messenger and the Last Day. Souls are indeed as you have said and in the state that you have described, and there are reasons for this.

The Imām, the Proof of Islam, attributed such a state to his own noble soul in one of his treatises, but this was out of humility, may God have mercy on him and grant us to benefit from him.

In short, one should make battle with such a soul, never neglect to discipline, alert, and remind it, and illuminate its darkness with the lights of sincere acts of worship and continuous remembrance.

As for the states that you say occur to the remembering disciple, the last [mentioned] which begins with languor and ends with slumber is a noble state and there are no states of true remembrance beyond it except one, which is the state of contemplation. He should be advised to persevere and continue with truthfulness and sincerity, seeking the highest Truth, for no other reason or motive save to establish his pure servitude before God's Lordship. Only such singleness of direction and purpose can avail under those circumstances. Your Lord is the Opener, the Omniscient, the Bestower, and the Generous.

48

'Abdallāh ibn al-Haytham asked him about the meaning of the word 'spontaneity', as well as about the saying of the common people: "For the sake of Monday, the key to the two doors."

He answered: As for you 'Abdallāh, a letter answering your first letter was sent to you containing the explanation of the word you inquired about in the *du'ā'* of the Beloved (may blessings and peace be upon him) but perhaps it has failed to reach you. *'Uqbā* means return, that is: "It is to You [O God] that the one who seeks [Your] good pleasure must [continually] return, until You are pleased."

As for spontaneous behavior (*badīha*), it is whatever a person does or says without prior reflection. When he does the right thing purposely he is said to be of good spontaneous behavior [or presence of mind], and when he fails to do the correct thing or just happens to do it by chance he is dispraised for his poor spontaneity and censured for having neglected to reflect and ponder [before acting].

As for the commoners saying: "For the sake of Monday, the key to the two doors," know that most of those sayings which you frequently hear from the commoners escape being measured by the criteria of either Law or reason. Should a man of wisdom wish to force upon these words an interpretation that is to a certain extent correct he might be able to find one. Monday is the day when deeds are reviewed [by God], one of the two doors may therefore be taken to be that through which they are presented and it will thus be open before them, the other to be the door through which passes the assistance (*madad*), descending toward those whose deeds were accepted and it will thus be open before it. Or one of the two doors may be taken to be that of the Prophet's entry into the world (may God's blessings and peace be upon him) and the other that of his exit from it. For he was born on a Monday (may blessings and peace be upon him) and died on a Monday. There are numerous other venues for interpretation.

49

> 'Īsā ibn Aḥmad Bā-Ḥadramī asked him about the relative merits of poverty and wealth and the seeming contradictions that exist in the *ḥadiths* concerning them.

He answered: In the Name of God the Merciful and Compassionate. Praise belongs to God Who made poverty the adornment of His virtuous servants and the embellishment of His successful elite. However, this is only so when it is accompanied on their part with contentment, submission, thankfulness and patient endurance of whatever hardships the August, the Omniscient imposes upon them. But when it is accompanied with panic, resentment, and objection to what destiny has brought, then it becomes a great affliction which leads to perpetual torment. Thus, whatever praise of poverty is to be found in the Book and *Sunna* refers to that poverty which is accompanied by patience, contentment and the maintenance of perfect courtesy with God the Exalted. An example of this is his saying (may God's blessings and peace be upon him): "Poverty is more embellishing to the believer than a beautiful harness on a horse's cheek." Whatever disparagement of poverty is to be found refers to that poverty which is accompanied by anger with destiny and resentment at how things were made to happen. This kind may lead its man to object to God's management of His creatures' affairs and to it refers his saying (may blessings and peace be upon him): "Poverty is not far from becoming disbelief."

Because poverty is more likely than wealth to lead to salvation and success both in this world and the next, it has been the choice of the most venerable of people, the Prophets and the saints, both in ancient and more recent times. For the poor man, when contented and thankful, has a status with God (Transcendent is He) that the wealthy never achieves even were he to give both himself and his wealth away for the sake of his Lord, Exalted is He. On the other hand the poor man, when resentful, becomes worse than the worst of the rich people, for his affliction would thus consist in objecting to God the Exalted and this is a horrendous matter, whereas the affliction of the rich is to be deceived by the world and indulge in enjoying it in a reprehensible manner.

This is the answer to your question so do understand it. May God bless our master Muhammad, his family and Companions, and grant them peace.

50

He also asked him about the prolongation of some peoples' lifespans as mentioned in some *ḥadiths*.

He answered: It has been soundly transmitted that a lifespan is a thing predestined and subject to neither prolongation nor shortening. Scholars (may God the Exalted have mercy on them) have disagreed on the meaning of the mentioned prolongation. Some of them chose the immediate meaning of the *ḥadiths* and stated that both prolongation and shortening depend upon certain conditions; for instance, if the lifespan of a man is so many years and he did such and such a thing it would be prolonged by so much. The same may be said about shortening and there are indications to that effect in tradition. But ibn 'Abbās (may God be pleased with him) said: "A man has a lifespan in this world from his birth to his death and another in the intermediary world from his death to his resurrection; both are preordained. When he obeys God the Exalted his worldly life is prolonged at the expense of his intermediary one, but when he contravenes and sins it is shortened and his intermediary life prolonged. Thus, the prolongation will not be from an external source and the preordained span will not be altered." And this is what I hold to be correct.

Other people have said that the mentioned prolongation is that one's life would become blessed so that one man's shorter life would outweigh another's longer one without this prolongation being physical. The purpose of a long life is that it should suffice for one to increase the range of his good works, this has indeed occurred to that fortunate servant and it is thus a true prolongation and an effective increase. Reflect on this answer and give it its due.

51

Shaykh ʿAbdal-Raḥmān ibn ʿAbdallāh ʿAbbād al-Shibāmī asked him about the utterance of Shaykh Abū ʿAbdallāh al-Qurashī: "The soul falls back on its habits when hardships come..."

He answered: Know that the soul in this and similar contexts is that subtle body which is inclined to enjoy the world's pleasures. The soul is such only in the traveler who is yet to be firmly established in his traveling, the superficial scholar and the heedless common man. Such souls undoubtedly resort to their habitual ways and means when afflicted with hardship because they concentrate wholly on them to the exclusion of all else and only take refuge in God as a last resort when they see that no assistance is forthcoming from the material worlds. On the other hand, the firmly established traveler and the gnostic who has reached God the Exalted have little soul to speak of, for these are either 'serene', that is submissive to the truth, and dominated by the power of the spirit, or else imprisoned and vanquished, possessing neither the power to act nor to move. So do understand!

As for a man to be subject to human weaknesses, this is something that appears at times and disappears at others but is never totally abolished, for God has a subtle secret in maintaining it and this is indicated by the things that happen to the great men and reveal its presence. It is often so well hidden that it gives the impression that it has gone altogether, [for example] in the stations of reliance (*tawakkul*), love (*maḥabba*), and the states of the 'truth' as well as the 'eye of certainty', and in other states which come under these. As for the 'knowledge of certainty' its possessor mostly resorts to his habitual means first before being eventually led back by his knowledge to God, Transcendent and Exalted is He. The important thing is for a man to seek refuge in God spontaneously when stricken with sudden hardship, without thinking, calculating, or relying on worldly means. When he does use some of these instead of [relying on] Divine management, he should use them outwardly while his heart and secret remain with God to Whom all matters return, in Whose Hand is all good, and Who has power over all things.

Meditate on this answer for it is of high value and, brief as it is, draws attention to things which would otherwise require much clarification and elaboration. "*God says the truth and guides to the path.*" [33:4]

52

> The jurist (*faqīh*) Muḥammad ibn 'Abdal-Raḥmān Mazrū' (may God's mercy be upon him) asked him: "Is it permissible for one who has yet to attain to the noble stations such as hope, love, and contentment to constrain himself to act according to them?"

He answered: Know, may God the Exalted be your teacher, that for one who neither possesses a sound state nor a firmly established station to act according to them is neither within the servant's power or choice, not even if by wishful thinking he imagines it to be so. [Furthermore] he would then be in danger of falling into the evil of false claims. That which is within one's power and choice is to wish to attain to them and travel the road that was opened by God the Exalted. These matters were excellently explained in the "*Iḥyā'*" and other books of the Proof of Islam (may God the Exalted have mercy on him).

A person may bring to himself [a state of] hope or contentment by thinking of what was said about them, should one of these states then occur to him he may act accordingly. There are states that alight on the heart without one having tried to cause or expose himself to them; when these occur one acts accordingly, whether one wishes or not. Know this! All the paper [in the world] would not suffice should we wish to elaborate further on this.

53

> He also asked him: "Is it permissible for one who fears ostentation to refrain from enjoining good and forbidding evil?"

He answered: This is under no circumstance permissible! He must strive against his ego to remove ostentation even as he acts, not by abandoning action for that is Satan's wish. [Abandoning action] was itself called ostentation by al-Fuḍayl, may God the Exalted have mercy on him and grant us to benefit from him: "To abandon action because of people is ostentation and to act for their sake is idolatry!" So long as one fears ostentation he is likely to remain a long distance from it. That which is beyond his control, that is, the thoughts that cross his heart, are requited by his loathing them whenever they are evil.

54

> The good Shaykh 'Abdal-Raḥmān ibn 'Abdallāh 'Abbād asked him whether the Proof of Islam ever mentioned the 'knowledge', 'eye' and 'truth of certainty' in the manner that the People (*al-Qawm*) discourse on them?

He answered: I have never come across this; however, the "*Iḥyā'*" and other writings of his do contain in various places references to these terms. The example you say was given by him about 'being informed that Zayd was in the house,' etc[26] ... is an explicit reference to the three ranks even though they were not explicitly named. The knowledge of Zayd is the first of them. And God knows best.

55

He also asked him: "Is it permissible for a man to attract to himself noble stations and states by reflecting on them in such a manner as to bring them on to a certain extent?"

He answered: Yes, it is. And reflecting on them is one way of reaching them, on condition that he does behave as is dictated by his reflection and joins practice to the reflection that requires it. To give an example, hope is one of the stations that a servant may reach by reflection on the verses and *ḥadiths* relating to it and performing those devotions that God the Exalted has made necessary if one is to reach it. You can apply this example in a similar manner to other stations.

As for states, these are gifts. Reflecting on them and other similar activities are a way of preparing oneself for them, after which they may or may not come. They may also come as a pure favor to one who is unprepared.

56

The same Shaykh also asked him about the utterance of Shaykh Abū-'Abdallāh al-Qurashī (may God be pleased with him): "Listening, then understanding, then arriving, then tasting."

He answered: Arriving is to tasting what listening is to understanding. When you hear a person describe a land and the wondrous things in it, this is listening. Understanding is to assimilate what he has told you. Arrival is to reach the land that was described to you. And tasting is to see and enjoy the wondrous things in it. He thus made use of that which is visible to indicate that which is not.

57

He also asked him about his statement in one of his treatises that a shaykh may refine a disciple (*murīd*) without the latter being aware of it.

He answered: This is so. The [kind of] shaykh meant here is the Shaykh of the Opening (*Shaykh al-Fatḥ*) who [spiritually] refines the disciple with thorough solicitude and wise care. There are two other kinds of shaykhs, the first is the shaykh of discipline and courtesy, and the second, less important one, the shaykh who provides [formal] teaching and [other] profitable things. These last two need to be known in person, respected, and firmly believed to be worthy of their task.

Shaykh Abul-Ḥasan al-Shādhilī exemplifies the "Shaykh of the Opening" that we have described. When he first met his disciple, Shaykh Abul-'Abbās al-Mursī, he told him: "You were made known to me ten years ago," or perhaps he may have said nine. Another example is that of *sayyid* Yūsuf of Fez with my master Shaykh Abū-Bakr ibn Sālim 'Alawī, may God be pleased with them and give us of their support. While he was still in Morocco and before he ever came to Hadramawt to meet him, Shaykh Abū Bakr visited him there. He evidently knew him and was able to describe him to others even as *sayyid* Yūsuf was still going from one shaykh to another in Morocco, unaware of who the shaykh who was looking after him was, until one of them swore to him that his shaykh was not in the Western provinces at all. And there are numerous other similar stories.

All three degrees may on rare occasions be united in one man who then becomes the "Absolute Shaykh" (*al-Shaykh al-Mutlaq*), the "precious elixir", and the "red sulphur" that is talked about but seldom found.

However, God's grace is vast and His generosity all-enveloping. Even when the Path is obliterated and its stars disappear, the [Divine] Ability remains operative and the domain of possibility is vast. It is not impossible, in this blessed time, to find one in whom God has united the three degrees, towards whom He leads those of His servants for whom He has willed good fortune, whom He makes known to those of His creation whom He wishes to raise to the degrees of sainthood. "*That is God's grace which He bestows upon whom He will, and God's grace is immense.*" [57:21]

Reflect deeply on this letter, may God grant you success, for it is of great value. And whenever you read it be full of reverence and true acceptance, free yourself from any claim to knowledge, and garb yourself in your confession that your comprehension lacks all penetration. This will make Satan despair of you.

58

> Shaykh 'Abdal-Raḥmān 'Abbād also asked him about the meaning of the term "erase" in the utterance of Shaykh al-Sūdī: "Erase all sciences and all that you used to write, for to erase them from all writing is necessary." And the jurist 'Umar asked him whether this was identical with what the Proof of Islam mentions in the chapter on Marvels (*al-'Ajā'ib*)[27] in the "*Iḥyā*'" in the context of the veils that prevent the heart from the unequivocal contemplation of the truth?

He answered: "Erasure" here has a meaning different from that mentioned by the Proof. To explain: The said sciences are the experiences and images that the heart contains. The erasure that the People speak about has two meanings. The first is to erase every experience, image or thought that comes into the heart and distracts it from being totally absorbed in its wayfaring to God the Exalted. This should happen in the beginning, and no traveler completes his traveling without it. The second is on arrival to the state of extinction and it is to erase all memories, thoughts, images, or any other thing to which the heart may possibly become attached or even simply attend to. It is to concentrate one's aspiration wholly on God the Exalted so that nothing remains in the heart but the remembrance of God (Majestic and August is He) and the will to head towards Him, Exalted is He. Erasure in this context means that one avoids relying and depending on "things" and strives to remove all attachment to them that may exist in the heart. This is accomplished by sheer effort at the beginning and until such time as it becomes one's state, and that is the state of extinction. In that state all things which divert one away from God the Exalted and are beyond one's control are obliterated. The person in such a state is absent, aware of nothing other that God the Exalted, not even of himself and of his own state of extinction. This is something to be experienced and not acquired by way of learning. Beyond this is the state of subsistence, and this is for those whom God has destined for leadership and rendered worthy of the vicegerency (*khilāfa*). Obliteration is thus followed by confirmation in a manner which neither distracts one from God the Exalted nor prevents the total dedication of the heart to Him.

As for that which the Proof wrote (may God the Exalted have mercy on him) concerning that which veils the heart, that is, his statement that the heart may be veiled from the clear vision of the truth by "following"; if he means following those who missed the truth in their endeavors, then the meaning is clear. But if he means following the independent scholars (*mujtahidūn*) who did arrive to the truth, then many meanings are possible: one is that those who speak the truth may utter some of its aspects and keep silent about others which were nevertheless necessary to mention. Another is that the truth he speaks may be expressed in a simplified manner to be clear to the common believers to whom God the Exalted has given him as a leader. "Following" as in those two examples, prevents the unveiled perception of the truth, which is the vision of things as they are with God the Exalted, [i.e., objectively] which is the attribute of Prophethood and sainthood. No person is required by law to worship God in this manner [since this is possible only for the elect]. Such following neither detracts from one's faith nor prevents anyone who dies a believer from attaining to salvation and entering the Garden. All independent scholars are correct and all believers who follow the leading religious scholars are rightly guided by their Lord. But one must distinguish between faith and knowledge on the one hand and unveiling (*kashf*) and inner vision (*baṣīra*) on the other, and between salvation and reward on the one hand, and beatitude and the [Divine] vision on the other. There are remote depths and obscure secrets in this matter, and the one who discourses on such sciences before those who have reached none of them by way of direct experience will only render them even more obscure by his explanations. We have said enough to solve the problem, God the Exalted willing, so reflect on it as it deserves.

59

> The venerable *sayyid* 'Īsā ibn Muḥammad al-Ḥabashī asked him whether the saying of the Messenger of God (may God's blessings and peace be upon him and his family): "A man is with whom he loves," was unconditional and thus applicable even to those whose words and deeds are dissimilar?

He answered: Know (may God the Exalted be your teacher) that this *ḥadith* induces both hope and alarm, for a man is with whom he loves whether they be righteous or depraved, what then of those who love the "accursed world"[28] and are thus with it? The togetherness which is the consequence of love will inevitably occur. However, love cannot be present unless one conforms to the beloved's acts and abstentions as far as possible. Love is a claim that can be established only with the proof of such conformity. The one who claims to love a person but diverges from him in those of his aims and desires which are within his power, who neither supports those whom he supports nor shows hostility to those he is hostile to, will logically be deemed to be untrue. True, it is not necessary to conform to the beloved in all his actions for this togetherness to occur, for then one would become effectively equal in everything where such equality is possible. Know then that love can never be without such conformity.

60

> The same *sayyid* questioned him about al-Muḥāsibī's utterance: "Each worshipper has his slackening spell and falls back either on a *Sunna* or an innovation."

He answered: I believe I have heard such a saying attributed to the Messenger of God (may blessings and peace be upon him). It means that a worshipper has in his beginnings so much determination in worship that it exceeds the limits of economy and of the norm enjoined on the generality of Muslims. If he becomes firmly established in this and is not led into harming his mind or body in a way that is legally reprehensible, then this is for him a kind of perfection. The worshipper then goes through a period of slackness when he falls below that level and if this is followed by a return to the prescribed pattern of economy then he has returned to the *Sunna*, but if he becomes wasteful by neglecting and shunning his devotions, then he has fallen back into innovation. Let us give an example to clarify: when a man feels himself driven to worship and devote himself to God the Exalted he may keep all-night vigils. He will then inevitably slacken up because of the human nature according to which he was made; if he then retreats from all-night vigils into keeping half or one third of the night he has achieved the *Sunna*, but if he abandons it altogether then he has fallen into innovation. The meaning of innovation in this context is deviation from the pattern of the virtuous predecessors. Slackness seems to affect the majority but not all worshippers. One should not refrain from initiating any regular devotion for fear of eventually slackening up, for that would be foolishness and self deceit.

61

Aḥmad ibn ʿAlī ibn Zuʿfa of al-Shiḥr asked him about the rules of isolation (*ʿuzla*) and retreat (*khalwa*) as well as other things.

He answered: Know (may God the Exalted be your teacher) that isolation is a more comprehensive term than retreat. Its aim is to be safe from evil and evil people. There are conditions to it, the most important of which are: to acquire the necessary sciences of *īmān* (i.e. faith) and *Islām* (i.e., doctrine and practice), that one's motive should not be his thinking-ill of other Muslims but his wish to preserve his religion, and that together with this, one should be wary of one's own ego and anxious not to allow its evil to harm other Muslims. Other conditions are for the one who isolates himself not to abandon the Friday or other congregational prayers, nor to neglect any of the duties imposed on him by God the Exalted towards other people or his own family and not to abandon the company of those people of goodness who would be of religious benefit to him. Imām al-Ghazālī (may God have mercy on him and grant others to benefit from him) has written convincingly on isolation in his book "*Minhāj al-ʿĀbidīn*" (The Method of the Worshippers), so do peruse it.

As for retreat, it is more specific than isolation and its aim is to refine the soul and polish the mirror of the heart so that the veil between oneself and one's Lord (Transcendent and Exalted is He) may be removed and all attachments to creatures severed so that no attentiveness to other than God the Exalted remains. Its conditions are the same as those of isolation with the addition that one must not enter it except with a realized shaykh. However, if [such a shaykh] is not found but the disciple is possessed of enlightened insight, powerful determination, strength of soul and exceedingly firm composure he is permitted to enter it. Its length is usually forty days and that is why it was called "*al-Arbe'īniyya*" (see glossary). However, it may be of ten, seven, or three days. I have seen a realized man make a disciple remain in seclusion for a hundred and twenty days. It seems to vary with the variations in the degree of purity or opaqueness of different people and with the differences between shaykhs. Suhrawardī (may God the Exalted have mercy on him and spread his benefit) has devoted elaborate chapters to it and you can read it if you wish. My master Shaykh 'Abdallāh ibn Abū-Bakr al-'Aydarūs (may God the Exalted have mercy on him and spread his benefit) often used to mention a brief seclusion where the disciple keeps secluded the night before Friday and the day while keeping to hunger, wakefulness, silence, isolation from people, absorption and concentration on God the Exalted and devotion to remembrance and the recitation [of the Qur'ān]. If you feel inclined to follow this pattern [then do] for it is blessed and profitable. The shaykh (may God the Exalted spread his benefit) is one of the most venerable of realized men, aware of many of the secrets of the path of God which had in previous days been hidden from others.

62

The same man also asked him about whether the experiences and unveilings of the gnostics were continuous or occurred only in certain states?

He answered: It seems that no unveiling of [Divine] Majesty or Beauty persists for very long; however, when it does, it abolishes the servant's discernment and renders him unaware of himself and of his own human nature. This [state] occurs to some people for a length of time and then departs. When obligatory devotions, such as prayers and fasts, are missed due to such a state of absorption, then they must be requited (*Qaḍā'*) at a later time.

It is the state of the traveler that higher realities appear to him at times and are veiled from him at others, and he remains so until he joins the masters (*mutamakkinūn*), then his state becomes such that creation does not distract him from the Real, neither does *ḥaqīqa* lead him out of the [boundaries of] *sharī'a*, nor does *sharī'a* veil him from *ḥaqīqa*. Some of those realities become permanently unveiled for him, while others are veiled at times and unveiled at others. Such a man attends to his daily life and engages in earning and industry, but these neither detract anything from him nor veil him from his Lord.

63

The same man also asked whether it was better for the disciple to remain near the shaykh or frequently to visit him?

He answered: If the shaykh gives him an indication as to which of these two he should do, then he should comply and firmly maintain himself in that condition. If he finds that any ill feelings have arisen within him because of this advice he should reveal all his affairs to the shaykh, especially those concerning the path and the state of his heart, neither awe nor modesty should prevent him from doing so. If his shaykh gives him no indication as to whether or not he should live with him, he is to do what is best for his heart and his respect and good opinion of his shaykh. Those succeed who abide by the shaykh's choice, raising no objection and preferring it to their own desires.

Should the disciple observe in his shaykh something which adversely affects his faith in him he should inquire about it. However, knowing the shaykh, if he thinks that he will not approve of such an inquiry then he must interpret it in an upright manner worthy of the status of God the Exalted's own people. As for those who, while said to belong to the path of God the Exalted, exhibit behavior that is not open to justification, such as adultery or appropriating other people's wealth unjustly, they fall under the laws ordained by God the Exalted for all Muslims, whether outwardly or inwardly. If it can be imagined that one such person has a disciple who learns from him in awareness [of what he has done] then he must believe that this was imposed on that servant by the writing of the Pen [i.e., destiny] and that he will return to God the Exalted with the kind of sincere repentance and true remorse that abolish the traces of sins and wash out their defilement. If, however, it becomes clear beyond suspicion or doubt that he is persisting in his sins and insolence with God the Exalted, then it has also become clear that he has been dispossessed and expelled by God (Transcendent is He) from His doorstep. He must then forsake and detest him for the sake of God the Exalted, for it is no small thing to be expelled from God the Exalted's doorstep, having been near [to Him], dispossessed after being given, and veiled after contemplating. God the Exalted does what He will. One should not think, however, that such ugliness of behavior can come from such people of the path who are known to belong to God the Exalted, have become prominent and well known to be under God the Exalted's protection, to receive His support and to have been chosen and drawn near to Him, for God guards them against such things and never allows [such things] to approach them [purely] out of grace and generosity. On the contrary, one who believes in them should believe that their hearts and their secrets contain limitless goodness, light, unveiling, sciences and wisdom out of which that which shows outwardly is no more than a grain of sand, a drop from the ocean. In this manner he will be much more able to benefit from them and their spiritual assistance to him will be greater.

May God grant us success in attaining soundness in both our intentions and acts and protect us from doubt and suspicion and bestow on us perfection in following His Messenger.

64

The scholarly Shaykh 'Abdal-Raḥmān ibn 'Abdallāh Bā-Rajā asked him about certain verses[29] by Shaykh Abū 'Alī al-Rūdhbārī (may God be pleased with him).

He answered: What we shall say is very brief.

As for his saying: "They said: 'Tomorrow is the feast, what will you wear?'", it is possible that 'they' refers to his brothers on the Path.

Their saying to him: "Tomorrow is the feast" is an indication that contemplation is to occur.

While his saying: "The gift of a pourer" may mean that He had bestowed upon him the Vice-Regency (*Khilāfa*). The pourer is the gnostic who pours the sciences and gnoses for the servants of God the Exalted to drink, by God the Exalted's order.

His saying: "Whose love I have quaffed" is a reference to the endurance of hardships on the path of God the Exalted and that those who revere their Lord greatly receive a great share.

The meaning of his saying: "No garb is more suited..." is to be found in this saying of the Prophet (may blessings and peace be upon him) on behalf of God the Exalted: "Those who draw nearer to Me do so with nothing better than that which I made obligatory on them..."[30] etc.

As for his saying: "Poverty and fortitude (*ṣabr*) are the two garments," the garment of poverty is the bestowal of pure slavehood and the garment of fortitude is one that is worn by all those who know the world; it is removed at the time of death.

His saying: "A heart beholding its comfort in Feasts and Fridays," bears two interpretations, the first and more likely one is that he wishes to preserve his conformity with the Law while in the eye of realities and in this case the [Friday] reunions [for the prayer] and the feasts will be those that Muslims are familiar with. The second meaning refers to the hours of contemplation and the times of Presence that a certain gnostic once spoke about thus: "A serene moment with God the Exalted is better than a thousand accepted pilgrimages."

His saying: "Time passes in mourning in your absence," etc., was explained by Shaykh ibn 'Aṭā'illāh in the "*Ḥikam*" thus: "Felicity, even though varied in its manifestations, is due only to the vision of Him and His nearness. And suffering, even though varied in its manifestations, is due only to the presence of His veil."

Shaykh Abū-Yazīd (may God be pleased with him and grant us to benefit from him) said: "In the garden are men who, were the Real to veil Himself from them for as long as the batting of any eyelid, would cry out to be saved from the Garden as those who are in the Fire cry out to be saved from the Fire."

These explanations are not complete; had we been granted permission to speak we would have given free rein to our pen, but to each thing its measure.

It is a remarkable coincidence that a few days before your letter arrived we had written to one of our friends in God the Exalted: "Know, my brother, that God (Transcendent and High is He) has servants whose feasts never end and to whom spiritual assistance never stops, because of the nights of nearness to their Lord which they experience in their hearts and the pleasure of intimacy in His Holy proximity. The feast is for them to maintain their conformity [to His Will], purify themselves from the soiling of disobedience, and be constantly present with God the Exalted at all times. One of them has said:

"Time passes in mourning in Your absence, O my hope!
The Feast is when You come to be seen and heard."

65

The scholar, Muḥammad ibn 'Abdal-Raḥmān Mazrū', asked him about certain thoughts that occurred to him and made him fear for himself.

He answered: Know that you will remedy these with nothing better than to ignore and forget them and whenever they occur repeat frequently, "*Subḥān al-Malik il-Khallāq*" (Transcendent is the Ever-Creating King.) "*in yasha' yudhhibqum wa ya'tī bikhalqin jadīd, wa mā dhālika 'ala'llāhi bi 'azīz.*" (If He wills, He can put you away and bring a new creation; that can be no great matter for God. Qur'ān 14:19,20) And know that these thoughts that force themselves upon you are of those afflictions that a believer is rewarded for when he maintains the courtesy due to the Real. They are allowed by God to afflict the servant so that, humbly and needfully, he may commit himself to Him and then He will answer: "*Is it not He Who answers those in need and removes evil*?" [27:62] Thoughts may result from such acts of the person as eating unlawful food or mixing with an evil person. So he must pass himself under scrutiny and repent from any such thing that he may find. If he suspects something wrong in himself but is unable to locate it, let him repent from all sins, those that he is aware of and those that he is not.

If thoughts may be conceived to occur without cause, then they should be regarded as pure afflictions and one should patiently endure them until their time ends by the Will of God the Exalted.

66

> The same man also asked him whether the reward for remaining seated after the dawn prayer at the same place where one has prayed until sunrise depends on remaining there, or would also be obtained by those who rise and either go home or somewhere else while maintaining uninterrupted invocation and *tasbīḥ*.

He answered: Know that the reward said to be due for remembering God the Exalted from after the dawn prayer until the sun rises has for a condition, in some *ḥadiths*, that one remain seated where one has prayed, while in others it is stated unconditionally. Remaining in one's place was mentioned by the Prophet (may blessings and peace be upon him) because it is more conducive to maintaining concentration [in *dhikr*] and avoiding dispersion. Those who keep to [the *dhikr*] and remain collected will inevitably receive their reward, whether they remain seated in their places or rise, especially if rising from it was prompted by one's care to increase in collectedness in *dhikr* by avoiding certain things in that place such as ostentation or loud voices. The same applies if one were to move for a matter involving an increase in goodness and benevolence, while maintaining [*dhikr*] and persevering in it. If, however, one leaves prompted by some desire such as a worldly matter or a pleasure such as coffee, then, as it appears, no reward will be obtained. Similarly [the reward is lost] if the said sitting was mentioned [in *ḥadith*] for some quality specific to it [and unknown to us]. The secrets of Prophethood, the subtleties of its meanings and the particularities of its perception are difficult to grasp comprehensively except by those who are established within it and this is a door that was closed by the death of the Messenger of God (may blessings and peace be upon him). Understanding is a vast ocean where each swims according to the share allotted him by his Lord. May God the Exalted grant us and you success in hitting the mark each time.

67

Shaykh 'Abdal-Raḥmān ibn 'Abdallāh 'Abbād asked him about the difference between powerlessness and weakness.

He answered: Know that powerlessness is the dwindling of the ability to either do or refrain from doing something to the extent that no such power remains. If one has the ability to do part of the whole thing then he is said to be able with regard to that part and powerless with regard to the rest. Powerlessness is the opposite of ability, while weakness is the opposite of strength; and strength is a part of ability. Weakness is thus incomplete ability so that the one who is able to achieve parts but not the whole of some activity is said to be weak; and God the Exalted knows best. Powerlessness is often used in common language for indolence which is the opposite of activity, that is, for a person to refrain, out of negligence and sluggishness from either doing or not doing something which is within his ability. These are my thoughts on the matter; I have referred to no books. May peace be upon you.

68

The *sayyid* Aḥmad ibn 'Awaḍ Bā-Ḥusayn asked him who of the two was superior to the other, Shaykh 'Abdal-Qādir al-Jīlānī or Imām al-Faqīh al-Muqaddam Muḥammad ibn 'Alī 'Alawī.

He answered: Know, may God the Exalted be your teacher, that Shaykh 'Abdal-Qādir (may God be pleased with him) is one of those to whom God gave both outward and inward knowledge, the practice of the method (*ṭarīqa*), the contemplation of reality (*ḥaqīqa*), and the education of disciples (*murīds*). He became the *Quṭb* and *Ghawth* of his time, and this was confirmed by many authorities. He died many years before our master and leader Muḥammad ibn 'Ali 'Alawi (may God be pleased with him), who was the shaykh of both method and reality, the leader of both the people of the outward and those of the inward, the Lordly Pole (*al-Quṭb al-Rabbānī*), the Foremost Jurist (al-Faqīh al-Muqaddam), and it is on him, after God and His Messenger, that we depend. Both were great leaders (may God be pleased with them), they were most comprehensive poles, *sunnī sharīfs*, and both are among the superior, outstripping, and drawn-nigh men. However, our benefiting and depending on *al-sayyid al Muqaddam* is greater and more in evidence because of his being both a father and a shaykh, as well as being the one around whom everything in this region revolves whether for us or for others. Similarly, Shaykh Abū Madyan (may God be pleased with him) was a great comprehensive leader who, according to certain gnostics, was made a Pole. Thus Polehood was transferred from Shaykh 'Abdal-Qādir to Shaykh Abū Madyan then to al-Faqīh al-Muqaddam in this order but not in immediate succession. The time period was long and many Poles may have intervened between each of them and the other. God, Transcendent and Exalted is He, knows better the reality of these matters. Our master the Shaykh and leader 'Abdal-Raḥmān ibn Muḥammad al-Saqqāf has said: "Next to the Companions we concede superiority to no one over al-Faqīh al-Muqaddam, except those whose superiority was explicitly stated (by the Prophet, may blessings and peace be upon him)." May God the Exalted be pleased with them all, and with us for their sake, and may He grant us spiritual assistance through them!

69

The same *sayyid* also asked him: "Who is the disciple (*murīd*)? Who is the Sufi and what is Sufism? And what does a man do to become a Sufi?"

He answered: Know that the disciple is he in whom the desire for the Face of God the Exalted and the Last Abode have totally overwhelmed his every outward and inward movement, whether for his worldly or after-life. This is a formidable matter when sound and firm, so reflect on it!

As for the Sufi, a certain gnostic once said that the Sufi was he who had become clear (*ṣāfī*) from turbidity, filled with the lessons of wisdom, freed by God the Exalted from needing others, and for whom gold and dust had become equal.

Sufism was said by another to be an "exit from every base attribute and entry into every sublime one." Much controversy has arisen between the people of the Path around what Sufism and the Sufi are, and what we have just quoted is among the best and most comprehensive [of what was said]. The complete or perfect Sufi is the one who purifies his actions, speech, intentions, and character from the blemishes of hypocrisy, and frees them from anything that might arouse the Master's[31] anger, who heads towards God the Exalted with the whole of his outward and inward, obeys Him, turns away from all others, detaches himself from all other preoccupations such as family, wealth, passionate desires, worldly things, and whims which are likely to distract him from devoting himself fully to this matter, and who then adds to this knowledge, adherence to the Book, *Sunna*, and example of the virtuous predecessors. And God, Transcendent and Exalted is He, knows best.

70

The same *sayyid* also asked him about *sulūk*, *munāzalāt*, and *iṣṭilām*, such as the people of the Path talk about.

He answered: *Sulūk,* or traveling, is the progression of the heart in the realization and reinforcing of the attributes of faith (*īmān*) and the stations and conditions of certitude, moving in that way from one position to another and ascending from one station to the next, from the beginning to the end. It is an inward movement on a inward path.

By *munāzalāt* they mean the divine inspirations which God bestows upon the secrets and the hearts.

As for *iṣṭilām*, they mean by it a powerful Divine *wārid* that overwhelms the servant to such an extent as to totally deprive him of his sensory perceptions and feelings. This is a rare occurrence and when it does happen it does not last for very long, however, when it does it makes its man join those ecstatics (*majdhūbs*) who are people of passionate love and exclusive attachment to God; and He knows best!

71

The scholarly *sayyid* ʻAbdal-Qādir ibn Muḥammad al-Ahdal the Yemeni the Ḥusaynī inquired about the practice of invoking blessings on the Messenger of God (may blessings and peace be upon him) after the Call to the ritual prayer (*adhān*) and about other things which will become apparent from the answer.

He answered: Your letter has arrived in which you mention that an argument took place concerning the *Mu'azzins* invoking blessings on the Messenger of God (may blessings and peace be upon him) after the Call and raising their voices in the manner that we are used to, that you quoted on this subject the words of Shaykh Ṣafiy al-Dīn ibn Ḥajar in his "*Sharḥ al-'Abāb*," and that some people raised objections to which you provided a reply in the form of that blessed essay which [we found] appropriate. May God reward you well. Then you quoted the straightforward question which you put to the shaykh, the man of purity, the *Muftī* of Islam Aḥmad ibn 'Umar al-Ḥubayshī and to which he gave a correct and profitable answer. May God reward his effort. You forwarded all of these to us together with the letter, I mean the quotation from Shaykh ibn Ḥajar, the study that follows it, the reply to the objection, and the said question and answer, and you requested us to give you what we had on that, for comfort and confirmation, although the study you made and the answer of Shaykh Aḥmad al-Ḥubayshī are evidently complete and sufficient. Therefore, it is only for the benediction and good omen that result from our speaking of the Messenger of God (may blessings and peace be upon him) and of his right, which can neither be ignored nor denied, that we say: His right upon his community (may blessings and peace be upon him) is the Greatest, and after that of God the Exalted, the most obliging and certain.

This right is impossible to fulfill whatever one may do or expend. There is nothing that is within our ability to attempt to fulfill this obligation except to conform to his *Sunna*, defend his religion, invoke blessings and peace upon him in abundance and have for him, his family, and his companions total love, attachment, honor and reverence.

As for invoking blessings and peace upon him, God the Exalted in His Noble Book commands His servants to do so by saying: "*God and His angels bless the Prophet, O believers bless him and invoke peace upon him.*"[32] [33:56] Numerous sound and strong *ḥadiths* were handed down exhorting to this and mentioning its merits, these are very well known everywhere, and so are the innumerable sayings of both ancient and recent men of God. Both are so familiar that there is no need to quote them. Shaykh ibn Ḥajar the second wrote a unique book on this subject which he called "*Al-Durr al-Manḍūd fil Ṣalāti wal'Salāmi 'alā Ṣāḥibi'l-Maqāmi'l-Maḥmūd*," (The Arrayed Pearls in Invoking Blessings and Peace on the Possessor of the Praiseworthy Station). Before him al-Sakhāwī wrote a book on the same subject, and the books of both the ancients and their successors among the community's leading scholars, particularly the books of *ḥadith*, are full of the same thing.

As for that which some *mu'azzins* do in some areas after giving the *adhān* for some or all the prayers, that is a good innovation, worthy of approval, which none can object to since we were commanded in the Book and *Sunna* to invoke blessings and peace upon the Messenger (may blessings and peace be upon him), and this was not confined to specific circumstances, time or place. Indeed some times and situations were expressly mentioned where reward is increased and the wage more generous, but the command and its merits remain valid at all times and situations, whether silently or aloud, alone or in a group. None of that can in itself be objected to and no objections can be raised without evidence [from the Book or *Sunna*] and no such evidence was ever transmitted. Therefore, their objecting statement must crumble and nothing remains with him to use as argument, for the time which follows the *adhān* is one where the invocation of blessings and peace on the Messenger is required, as is to be found in sound *ḥadiths*. That this is done loudly by the *mu'azzin* so that those who belong to the Prophet's community (may peace be upon him), whether those who are awake or those who are not, are reminded of it, is an increase in goodness and benefaction. This reminding of the invocation of blessings and peace on the Messenger of God (may blessings and peace be upon him) after the *adhān* in the manner that you mention is habitual to the inhabitants of the two Noble Sanctuaries before each prayer except Sunset (*Maghrib*) because of the lack of time and Dawn (*Subḥ*) where they do it before the *adhān*. It is also done in our country, Hadramawt, but not at all times and not in all areas, but were it to be done here after each *adhān,* I do not think that anyone would deny or object to it, for who would deny such a blessed act or object to it in itself? God forbid! Many *mu'azzins* also recite the noble verse that you mentioned "*God and His angels bless the Prophet...*" after the *adhān* is finished. There is no doubt that to mention him (may blessings and peace be upon him), to praise him, and relate his merits and virtues as that reminder does, together with invoking blessings and peace upon him, are among the greatest of devotions and the most important acts of worship. They strengthen and reinforce faith, and increase the love and reverence for the Messenger of God (may blessings and peace be upon him), in both the reminder and those believers who listen to him. They also enrage and humiliate those hypocrites and disbelievers who detest him, may the best of blessings and peace be upon him.

What possible excuse remains for the one who denies such an act with all its benefits and profits and other merits which God the Transcendent and Exalted, has promised those who invoke blessings and peace on His Messenger (may blessings and peace be upon him) such as that none among his community invokes blessings on him once but that God, Eminent and Majestic is He, blesses that person ten times, and the same for invoking peace? If the person who has objected has done so to the very idea of this kind of reminding, then he is ignorant and mistaken, of less consequence than to be addressed and too ignorant to be taught.

Nothing can be soundly understood
If daylight itself needs proof.

If he has objected to its being done after every *adhān* and the custom in your area is to do it at only some times such as after *Jumu'a* and so on, as is done over here, then his objection is natural for he would have objected to that which he is not used to and finds difficult to accept, and such things often happen with people of formalities, who are under the sway of habits and customs. If he has objected not to the matter in itself but because it disturbs people in prayer and other suchlike [activities] then if this is true he has a point. This is similar to reciting the Qur'ān aloud during audible prayers, as will not be difficult for you to see. You have not mentioned whether explicitly or implicitly who the man is who has raised the objection, what kind of person he is and of which rank.

There is a purpose in mentioning him and one's statements on the matter would differ accordingly, for some people are fanatics, others are jealous of the speaker and object, because of their envy, to that which they would not have objected to had it come from another person. Others affect ignorance and others still should not have been addressed in the first place. People are of many categories and it is of some use to specify [to which he belongs].

You have also not mentioned which kind of reminding is customary in your area, is it done at some of the [prayer] times or all of them after each *adhān*? There would have been some use in that also.

It may be that the objections of this man grew stronger after you gave him your answer, which is true but involves a certain amount of disparagement and humiliation. If that answer had been produced after you had explained to him with gentleness and subtlety and he had refused to accept then indulged in an excess of criticism and disparagement, then you were right and have done well, may God reward your effort. However, I advise you to be as subtle and gentle as possible whenever enjoining good or forbidding evil; in this manner [one's advice] is more likely to be accepted and more effective in settling seditious subjects and closing all doors to antagonism and division and it is this that we were ordered to do in the Law.

"Gentleness when present in anything embellishes it, and rudeness when present in anything disgraces it." (*ḥadith*) And it has also been transmitted that "God, Transcendent and Exalted is He, is Gentle and likes gentleness." There is nothing in gentleness that is not good.

72

> The scholarly Shaykh Aḥmad ibn Abū-Bakr Bā-Sha'bān Bā-Faḍl who lived and died in India asked him: "Why is backbiting considered in Islam to be worse than thirty adultery offences although it was not considered [by scholars] so full a major sin as adultery?"

He answered: This is not due to backbiting being worse than adultery as far as outward appearances are concerned, for adultery can be seen to be a depravity which leads to the confusion of lineages and other corruptions, but to the motive behind adultery being merely lust which is a bestial attribute, while the motive behind backbiting and dishonoring Muslims is malice in the heart and rancor and perfidy toward the [slandered] Muslim. These are demonic attributes and are up to thirty times worse and more loathsome than bestial attributes, as in the *ḥadith*, provided it is soundly transmitted. It has also been transmitted that backbiting is worse than adultery but no [specific] number was mentioned. The fact that backbiting, as relating to the rights of creatures, is worse than adultery is evident. It has been stated in a weak transmission that one *fals*[33] worth of injustice to

[God's] servants is redeemed by seven hundred accepted ritual prayers. The wronging of [God's] servants is that wrong which is never left [unpunished].

73

The same scholar also asked him about whether the believers among jinn had any share in the gnosis of the gnostics, and in the vision [of God] were they to enter the Garden.

He answered: Know that the gnostic Shaykh 'Abd al-Wahhāb al-Sha'rānī the Egyptian (may God the Exalted have mercy on him) has mentioned that jinn, meaning the believers among them, had a share in the elect's gnosis and that they had posed to him certain questions on that subject and he had written a book entitled: "*Kashf al-Rān 'an As'ilat al-Jān*" (*The Removal of the Veil from the Questions of the Jinns*) and I have indeed come across that book of his.

Concerning the vision of God the Exalted in the Garden, know that there are differences of opinion regarding whether the believers among jinn enter the Garden. It has been stated that no specific proof exists as to their believers entering the Garden and this view was supported only by generalities which were not accepted by those who held that they did enter it.

My opinion, and knowledge belongs to God, Eminent and Majestic is He, is that the believers among them enter the Garden, God the Exalted willing, and in it behold the Lord.

74

The same man also asked him what a man who has no progeny should keep in mind when praying for his *dhurriyya*.

He answered: The word *dhurriyya* is used to designate one's children and their descendants and one's parents [or ancestors] however far back they go. An example of the second instance is His saying, Exalted is He: "*And a sign for them is that we carried their* dhurriyya *in the laden ship*." [36:44] When a man who has no *dhurriyya* according to the first meaning prays he should intend all his ancestors and also his descendants, for if he is without children at that time they are still within the realm of the possible. It is hardly conceivable that a living human being, even though impotent, may be definitely certain that he will have no descendants in the future, for the possibility remains open to him; it only becomes impossible when he dies. There is no harm for a childless man to pray for his children and mean his siblings' and near relatives' children for they are as if his own. Similarly, a scholar of virtue may intend by his prayer those who learn from him and follow his example. And God - Transcendent is He - knows best.

75

The same man also asked him about the sprouting of people before the resurrection.

He answered: It seems that they will be outside the earth but connected to it like plants. There is no contradiction between this and His saying, Exalted is He: "*Then when He calls you once, out of the earth you shall come forth*." [30:25] For what is meant here is a second coming forth with spirits and bodies "*... running with outstretched necks to the Caller*," and that is different from the first coming forth.[34] Similarly, there is nothing unlikely in their standing on the Bridge after the earth is changed, if the tradition relating to that is sound, for it will then stand there and God the Exalted may, should He so wish, enlarge it then render it very thin so that the crossing becomes a trial and a test of sincerity. The term Bridge may also designate things other than that which overhang Hell, may God the Exalted protect us and you from it. The matter is vast, the Dominion of God the Exalted vaster, and Divine Ability and Knowledge vaster still.

76

> The same man also asked him about how a man can enter the Garden from all eight gates.

He answered: If the gates are scattered along the Garden's surrounding wall he will enter from one of them and the others will be open for him as an honor and an added dignity. That is they will all be open for him to enter from whichever he chooses. I have seen this mentioned by some scholars, may God the Exalted show them Mercy. The *ḥadith* concerning what is to be said after the ritual purification (*wuḍū'*) says: "The eight gates of the Garden are open for him to enter from whichever he chooses." Do look it up for the meaning there is clear and it is that which is easier to understand. And if the gates are one on each of the Garden's degrees and these are eight, each tier above the other, then the meaning would be that he has reached the highest Garden by going through all of the eight gates which are those of the Garden's tiers. And God, Transcendent and Exalted is He, knows best.

77

> The same man also asked whether the *ḥadiths* concerning the resurrection of arrogant people in the form of small specks of dust and that of others in forms equivalent to those ugly attributes which were theirs in the world should be taken at face value or had other meanings.

He answered: There is nothing to prevent this from happening as described and one should not incline toward other meanings when it is possible for it to occur as in the mentioned *ḥadiths*. When the Prophet was asked (may blessings and peace be upon him) how the damned would walk on their faces to the Fire he said: "The One who made them walk on their feet is able to make them walk on their faces." Therefore, understand that what is meant here is the vastness of Divine Ability unless the matter involves that which is considered either by the intellect or the Law to be impossible.

78

> He also asked him about the saying of our master Imām al-Ghazālī (may God have mercy on him and make us benefit from him and his books): "Not everyone has a heart."

He answered: He meant (may God show him Mercy and make others benefit from him) the real heart that understands and comprehends what it receives from God the Exalted. This is a noble reality which finds its support in the formal heart of flesh which everyone has. To the same meaning do those words of God the Exalted refer: "*In that is a reminder to him who has a heart*" [50:37], that is, a heart that comprehends what it receives from God the Exalted. While in another verse He confirms their possession of the formal heart but denies them the comprehension which is the real purpose and aim of it, so He says, Exalted is He: "*They have hearts but comprehend not with them.*" [7:179]

This is what was given to quote at the present moment with no previous reflection or deliberation, it is the inspiration of the moment and the overflow of grace, the effect of the succor provided by the interpretation of the mystery of the meaning of "*... and We taught him of Our Knowledge.*" Everything that we have is from this Comprehensive Presence, had we wished we would have said much more but we have met with the time and epoch that you see and know. If there be one of the elect, he should be given according to the nature of his election and not subjected to the generalities appropriate for the common people. And let not momentary illusions prevent you from asking questions, even if these be many, for we shall answer whenever time allows as we should rightly do and in the manner that is most profitable and preferable. We shall thus be with you and you shall be with us in the best and most appropriate way in the unconditioned Presence.

79

The same man also asked him about the return of his spirit to him (may blessings and peace be upon him) whenever a Muslim of his community salutes him so that he may answer him, as in the *ḥadith*.

He answered: There is nothing obscure in that. It means that what returns is a certain faculty of the spirit concerned with the perception of the Messenger (may blessings and peace be upon him) of the salute of those of his community who salute him. Here a term was used to express part of its meaning, as is often done.

Some scholars have said that this return implies, of necessity, that his spirit (may blessings and peace be upon him) be continuously present in his noble body, because there is not one moment in existence without one of his community saluting him. This is a correct opinion but of limited scope compared with the scope of the people of vast inspirational sciences drawn from the Divine Presences. However, what we have mentioned will be sufficient by the Will of God the Exalted.

80

He also inquired about when the forms of the people of the Garden and those of the Fire will change into beauty or ugliness or the other attributes that were mentioned in *ḥadith*.

He answered: I believe, and God knows best, that it is after the Divine Judgment is passed, which will be based upon the people of the Garden having upheld the [Divine] commands and the people of the Fire having neglected them, that either the Garden or the Fire will become their inevitable fate. That is the time when each of the two groups will be sent to their final abode. It would be near enough to say that it is at the moment of their entry into the Garden or the Fire.

81

> He also asked him whether it was permissible for one man to have more than one shaykh, and about other matters as will be mentioned.

He answered him: The questions you have asked need a lengthy exposition which the present time does not allow, we shall therefore discourse on them in the briefest terms that will fulfill our purpose and clarify them.

Yes, it is permissible on condition that no contradiction or opposition exists between their respective methods (*ṭarīqas*), that no differences between them exist, and that they all be people of truthfulness and fair mindedness. Depending on just one is the reliably sound thing to do and is in most cases necessary. Were he to forbid you to meet others and take from them, this would become obligatory and to do otherwise would mean ruin since the success of the disciple may be dependent upon it. It does not become a disciple to do otherwise while still in his state of weakness at the beginning of his entering the path; this is more conducive to his heart being collected and his aspiration abundant. We have mentioned some of that toward the end of the "Book of the Disciple,"[35] so look it up there.

82

He also asked him about a certain ruling concerning audition (*Samā*‘) which will appear from the answer.

He answered: Audition, when in the presence of a shaykh who is a master, when the people attend with his permission and conform to the conditions he imposes on attenders and they all believe in the shaykh and raise no objections to him, then everyone present will be under the protection of his spiritual state, power of resolution and enveloping solicitude.

83

He also asked him about the first step that a disciple takes on the path of God the Exalted.

He answered: It is the step of repentance. There are other things which should precede and follow it. In the early chapters of the "Book of the Disciple" are indications to that effect.

84

He also asked him about what happens when the disciple commits himself entirely to the shaykh.

He answered: It is the shaykh's to consider his case and do what he considers best, more beneficial and elevating for him, for he is a trust that God the Exalted entrusted him with. The states of the disciples differ a great deal in that respect and the disciple has to accept whatever counsel the shaykh gives him and [whatever state] he establishes him in, whether outwardly or inwardly, without adding anything of his own volition.

85

He also asked him about the difference between the Unseen and the visible realms and about other things.

He answered: The Domain of the Visible (*'Ālam al-Shahāda*) is that which can be perceived through the five senses, whereas the Domain of the Unseen (*'Ālam al-Ghayb*) is that which lies beyond that. It is those things of God the Exalted which sound minds should accept, hearts possessed of certainty believe, and which the Prophets of God the Exalted and His Saints contemplate with their inner sight according to God the Exalted's will.

As for the worlds of the *Lāhūt*, *Nāsūt* and *Jabarūt*, the world of the *Lāhūt* (Divine Realm) is that part of the Unseen where nothing but purely Divine matters are to be seen. The world of the *Nāsūt* (Human Realm) is the part that opposes it, where subtle spiritual human matters are to be seen.

The world of the *Jabarūt* (Realm of Power) is that part of the Unseen where appear those Divine matters related to the realities of Invincibility, severe chastisement, swift revenge, the utmost in Loftiness and Independence and other such things.

This is in summary what we have understood and extracted from the leading authorities in this field. Understand it as it should be understood and reflect on it as it deserves. Success and assistance are granted by God.

86

> The scholarly Shaykh Aḥmad ibn 'Abdallāh Sharāhīl asked him: "Abū-Muḥammad Sahl ibn 'Abdallāh (may God the Exalted show him mercy) has said: 'Every act that the servant does, whether it be one of obedience or disobedience, without following an example, is sustenance for the soul, while each act done following an example is suffering to the soul,' how can one follow an example in disobedience?"

He answered: First of all, know that the term soul as used by the Sufis, may God make us benefit from them, refers to a subtle body in human beings, the nature of which is to prefer immediate comforts. It is by nature attracted to perishable things. What they mean by its "suffering" is to discipline it to conform to the Book and the *Sunna*, which is a condition for sound traveling (*sulūk*). This suffering is to battle with it to make it follow the truth, avoid falsehood, and shun all that is unnecessary. They consider this struggling to be [nothing but] felicity itself both immediate and as an end state. They only call it suffering as a concession to the level of ordinary people that they may understand what they mean. Since to closely follow the Messenger of God (may blessings and peace be upon him) is the very behavior which encompasses the totality of what is intended, the People (may God be pleased with them and make us benefit from them) are of all people those who show the greatest concern and care for it. They give no credit, may God allow people to benefit from them, to anyone whose activities or moments of stillness, both outward and inward, do not conform to the Book and *Sunna*. Sahl (may God show him mercy), by saying "Every act…" etc., is warning that to abandon conformity, even while engaged in doing something which the soul is not by its nature inclined to, such as obedience, strengthens and arouses its passionate desires, while every act that conforms [to the Book and *Sunna*] even if the act is one that the soul is by nature inclined to, such as sins and pleasurable but unnecessary things, puts it through the greatest hardship. That is because following the Messenger (may blessings and peace be upon him) is the truth. The truth is opposed to whimsical desire, and the soul is a prisoner of its desires; it tends to agree with them and is inclined to follow them. The soul is also, by virtue of a hidden secret, made to detest being forced by anyone into docility and submission and loves to be given a free rein in all matters and to act independently; it holds that none should have power over it. It therefore detests following anyone, even in that which accords with its own nature, and it tends not to conform, even in avoiding that which it is averse to, as we have mentioned before.

As for the meaning of following an example in disobedience, we must first, for the sake of courtesy, mention the meaning of following an example in obedience. In acts of obedience it means performing them solely for the sake of God the Exalted in a manner that conforms outwardly and inwardly to knowledge and courtesy. In permissible things it is to take and use whatever is to be used in the belief that it is lawful and the intention of using it to fulfill the rights of God the Exalted. In abandoning sins, it is to abandon them because one is ashamed before God the Exalted, in reverence for Him and in fear of His punishment. As for its meaning in committing sins, if his destiny is to commit them, it is not to do so deliberately, experience any joy or persist in them. It is also to hide them from people and make haste to repent to the King, the Real, fearful of being asked to account or be punished for them.

This is not a complete clarification of Sahl's words (may God make [people to] benefit from him) for they contain comprehensive meanings and profitable courtesies, but it is, by the Will of God the Exalted, informative and sufficient. The best of speech is that which is brief and informative. Any of their utterances can never be fully explained in less than a volume or more by those who are familiar with their sciences, so take heed, O people of insight! May God the Exalted grant us and you success in hitting the mark!

87

> The jurist (*faqīh*) Muḥammad ibn 'Abdal-Raḥmān Mazrū' (may God's mercy be on him) asked him why a person should be attached to creatures and how he can rid himself of it.

He answered: Know that its cause is weakness in one's certitude and the remedy to rid oneself of it is powerful certitude. This is achieved by two means: the first is to meditate on God's speaking indications (*āyāt*) which are the verses (*āyāt*) of the Book and His silent indications which are the wonders of existence in both higher and lower worlds. This is called reflection (*fikr*) by the people of realization. The second is to refine the soul and polish the heart's mirror by effective discipline and sincere effort (*jihād*) until the Real manifests itself in it, and this is the way that the Sufis prefer (may God have mercy on them all and grant us to benefit from them!). And do not think that certitude is firm belief, for that is possessed by the generality of believers yet their attachment to creatures is undiminished. The certitude referred to is a Divine light that envelopes the heart and takes hold of it so that its possessor desires nothing but God the Exalted and becomes indifferent to his own self, let alone all other worlds. One of the heart's effective remedies is to constantly remember that no creature is capable of bringing benefit or preventing harm to its own self; no helplessness could be greater, so how can a rational person become attached to such a one? These [attachments] can only be deceptions of the imagination indicating weakness of certitude. So busy yourself with strengthening your certitude that you may escape them.

88

> The same jurist also asked him: "How is it that one loves the virtuous (*ṣāliḥūn*) while neither emulating them nor following the path that made them become so?

He answered (may God be pleased with him and give us the realization of his sciences): Know that the benefit derived from loving them does not depend on emulating them in every way so that their every action is similarly performed, for the one who does that is none other than one of them and those who love him will then be counted among their lovers. However, the good that is dependent on loving them can only be won when some traces of emulating them begin to appear. As for not following their way, this is nothing but a lack of determination, for determination is the mould of success and success is in the treasury of God the Exalted, so ask Him for it.

89

> The same person also asked him: "Why does one like those who praise him, even if with that which is not his, and dislike those who criticize him, even if for that which is in him?"

He answered: Know that this thing is kneaded into the very nature of the Son of Adam, only those who have escaped from the necessities of their human nature and reached the level of the spiritual angels are safe from it. The way to do this was mentioned in the answer to the first question. To be safe from this, according to the people of sincerity, is to regard praise and dispraise, as well as the persons praising or dispraising one, as equal. As for disliking dispraise and liking praise, those can be either permissible or forbidden according to the reason. A man who is pleased with praise because it means that he is highly regarded by the other person, and is displeased with dispraise because it means that he is poorly regarded, is a man who is veiled and has a poor share of the elect's concentration. But one may be pleased with praise and displeased with dispraise with the thought that the tongues of creatures are the pens of the Real and that He, Transcendent is He, has revealed the [person's] beauty and concealed his ugliness. Such a man, when his good points are revealed and spoken about feels joy because of his hope that his Lord will treat him in the same manner [in the Hereafter] and when he is criticized and his bad points are revealed he is fearful that his Lord may treat him in the same manner in the Hereafter. To go deeper into this matter would require lengthy elaboration; the last part of it was fully expounded by the Proof of Islam in the chapter on dispraising prominence and ostentation in the "*Iḥyā'*."

90

A person asked him about the saying: "He who knows himself knows his Lord."

He answered: Know that this is a *ḥadith* transmitted from the Messenger of God (may blessings and peace be upon him). It contains, in its brevity, much knowledge and sciences, for he was (may blessings and peace be upon him) strengthened with [the gift of] comprehensive expression. Then know that this utterance has many meanings but we shall confine ourselves to briefly mention only two of them, God the Exalted has said: "*We shall show them Our signs on the horizons and in themselves till it is clear to them that it is the truth, Is it not enough for your Lord to be Witness over things*?" [41:53] and: "*In the earth are signs for those who possess certitude and in yourselves, can you not see*?" [51:20]

The first meaning of knowledge of oneself being the way to know the truth is that if you see your own incapacity, poverty, shortcomings, and helplessness and that you can neither bring benefit nor prevent harm to yourself, you will know that you have a Lord and Creator Who alone brought you into existence and gave you your strengths, Who will ask you to account for what you have acquired and will reward you according to your deeds, Who is limitlessly rich and Whose Existence is Real. A gnostic was asked: "How did you come to know your Lord?" He said: "By the breaking of resolutions," meaning that his resolution to do something might be followed by a failure to execute it and his resolution not to do something might be followed by it being done, this led him to conclude that he had a Lord and that his fate was [not in his own but] in someone else's hand and that that was God The Eminent, The Wise.

The second meaning is that when you observe your soul and see it inclined to evil and falsehood, turning away from good and truth, desirous of enjoying the ephemeral world, forgetful of the everlasting Hereafter, naturally drawn to fulfilling its lustful desires and falling under the yoke of habits, then you know that only its Creator can save you from its dangers, and protect you from its temptations, only He is able to reform it and that He is God, the Blessed and Exalted. Then you concentrate on Him, find Him sufficient, and depend on Him. When He sees, Transcendent is He, that in your heart you wish sincerely to flee to Him and that your desire for sincerity is sound, He will flood you with lights and reveal to you well guarded secrets. Into that soul of yours that incites to evil and is drawn to evil and evil doers, He will pour serenity and conformity to the truth, repugnance of falsehood, and the wish to pursue goodness and associate with the best of people, so much so that it will please your heart. He will erase from your heart everything that may distract you from traveling the path to proximity. Then you will know the gentleness of your Lord, Eminent and Majestic is He, and His care, acceptance, and solicitude for you. The root of this knowledge is the awareness of the ominous nature of the soul which leads you to run for protection to God the Exalted. So be aware of that and reflect on it as it deserves, and be content with this glimmer for it is of the hidden knowledge of the seas which are turbulent. That which we have mentioned should be informative and sufficient. "*To God do all things return.*"

91

Shaykh ʻAbdal-Raḥmān ibn ʻAbdallāh ʻAbbād, asked him about "audition" for those who have crossed the states and stations.

He answered: As for "audition" by those who have crossed the states and stations, it is mentioned by the "Proof" (al-Ghazālī) in the second chapter of the "Book of Audition" and he refers to those who are extinct to everything other than God the Exalted, even to themselves. The observable example of this occurring between created beings is that of the women cutting their hands at the sight of Joseph's beauty, they were truly extinct in contemplating him and thus unaware of themselves.

92

Aḥmad ibn Muḥammad al-Ghasham al-Zaydī[36] asked him how he stood with regard to the acts of created beings?

He answered: Know, may God grant you success, that our school, our belief which we hold before God the Exalted is that nothing good or evil, beneficial or harmful, happens other than by God's decree and will. That which He wills is and that which he does not is not. There are, to support this, more textual evidence from the Book and the *Sunna* and more logical proofs for anyone possessed of insight than can be numbered. The books that our leading [scholars] have written on the Principles of Religion overflow with these and they are in your hands. Our position is intermediary between two others, the first of which is that of the Fatalists (*Jabriyya*) who say that people are forced to act as they do, that they are, under all circumstances, subdued and overpowered, and that their actions are thus no different from those of the absent minded or the coerced, or even the insane or the sleeper. This position can be clearly seen to be rationally false, even if no proof is advanced to this effect. The second is the *Mu'tazilite* position that people's actions originate in them by choice, they act when they so wish and refrain when they so wish. Our position is what every person knows about himself, for no rational man is unaware of the difference between that part of his behavior which is inescapable and which he is forced into and that part which is by choice yet in which he is not altogether independent. The view that nothing whatsoever happens except by God's Will and decree must be our belief and no faith can be sound without it. We nevertheless like and praise obedient people, urge them to show more zeal in obedience, warn them against falling into disobedience, and hold that God the Exalted will reward them. And we dislike the disobedient, urge them away from sin and into obedience, and hold that God the Exalted will punish them. We carry out the statutory punishment (*ḥudūd*), present our complaints against injustice to the rulers, enjoin good and forbid evil. And we consider it to be one of the greatest sins for a sinner to reply when asked why he has sinned that it was God's will and decree. To accept contentedly God's decree is necessary with us and it means accepting everything that He does as favors from Him and justice. That the heart should remain serene when losses in lives or wealth occur or hardships and anxieties arise, we hold as a sign of contentment, whereas contentment with sins we hold as a major sin.

93

Al-Zaydī also questioned him about those Muslims who fought 'Alī (may God honor his countenance).

He answered: Know that those who rebelled against 'Alī (may God be pleased with him) and whom he personally made battle with during his caliphate were three groups:

The first are those who were present on the Day of the Camel[37], al-Zubayr, Talḥa and 'Ā'isha (may God be pleased with them all) and the people of Basra. They first gave allegiance, then rebelled against him, seeking revenge for the blood of 'Uthmān (may God be pleased with him). His assassination had neither been carried out, ordered, nor approved by 'Alī (may God be pleased with him), but he accepted the allegiance of those who had perpetrated it and did not turn them over, for the good of the faith and to maintain unity among Muslims at that time. These reasons were not understood by the rebels.

The second are those who were at Ṣiffīn[38], Mu'āwiya, 'Amr ibn al-'Āṣ, and the people of Syria. They had not sworn allegiance to 'Alī and they rebelled demanding revenge for 'Uthmān.

The third are those who were at Nahrawān, the *Khawārij*. They had given him their allegiance and fought with him, then rebelled in rejection of the arbitration that had taken place at Siffin.

None of those were fought by 'Alī (may God be pleased with him) before he had invited them to meet with him for conciliation and again to accept his authority, and they had refused to do so. In our view they are all people who have overstepped their limits, disputed [what was not theirs], and rebelled with no evident justification or clear right. However, those of them who rebelled for disputable reasons are better than those who disputed him his authority, desiring it for themselves. God is more aware of their intentions and inner thoughts, our safety lies in saying nothing about them, they are a community who has passed. Our scholars have stated that al-Zubayr and those who were with him, and Mu'āwiya and those who were with him, having exercised their judgment, made the wrong decisions, they are thus excusable. Anyhow, the most that can be said about those among the people of *Tawḥīd* who pray and pay their *zakāt*, but rebel against the head of the state is that they are sinners, and in our view we are not allowed to curse a sinner specifically. We do not consider it to amount to disbelief (*kufr*) to rebel against the leader, nor do we consider it permissible to curse a specified person except one whom we know died a disbeliever, under no circumstances to be reached by God's mercy, as for example the Devil. Having said that, there is still no virtue in cursing such people. We allow the cursing of sinners, transgressors and oppressors only in general.

As for Ḥasan and Ḥusayn (may God be pleased with them) they were leaders by right and indeed fulfilled the conditions of leadership and were perfectly worthy of it. To Ḥasan the "people of decision"[39] among those who were under Imām 'Alī swore allegiance, following the latter's assassination. When Mu'āwiya and the people of Syria marched against him he came out to meet them with the people of Iraq. When the two armies drew close to each other Hasan had compassion and pity for the community so that God fulfilled that which his grandfather (may blessings and peace be upon him) had said: "This son of mine is a *sayyid*, I hope that through him God the Exalted will bring conciliation between two large factions of Muslims." Ḥasan then deposed himself and pledged his allegiance to Mu'āwiya, having first imposed some conditions on him. He died (may God be pleased with him) before Mu'āwiya, the latter designated his son, Yazīd, as heir and the people gave him their allegiance either willingly or under coercion. Ḥusayn having refused him his allegiance, was written to by the people of Iraq who requested him to come to them and be their leader. He accepted and set out for Iraq. Yazīd then wrote to his deputy in Basra, 'Ubaydullāh ibn Ziyād, ordering him to march against Ḥusayn and defeat him. This he did and the people of Iraq let him do this even though they had at first claimed to pay allegiance to Ḥusayn. Ḥusayn was killed, a martyr together with some members of his household (may God be pleased with them all). Those who killed him, those who ordered it, and those who assisted in it we regard as transgressors and violators, may God treat them according to His justice[40]. Yazīd we do not regard as similar to Mu'āwiya, for Mu'āwiya (may God be pleased with him) was a Companion, he neither neglected his obligations nor committed offenses, whereas Yazīd was undoubtedly depraved, he abandoned his prayers, murdered people, committed adultery and drank alcohol. His judgment we leave to God the Exalted.

94

> He also asked about the gatherings held in mosques where love poetry is sung to the accompaniment of pleasant tunes and rhythmic melodies.

He said: Know that we consider those to amount neither to *dhikr* nor something similar, they are permissible but to abandon them is better. Poetry was recited in the presence of the Messenger of God (may God's blessings and peace be upon him), at his own bidding on occasions and he sometimes quoted one or two verses. It was recited in his mosque in his presence by Ḥassān[41] and others. The permissibility of a thing is established by it being done once, provided no order forbidding it follows. Although it was never recited accompanied with music in the presence of the Messenger of God (may blessings and peace be upon him), if it was allowed without such an accompaniment it should not be forbidden with it unless there is clear evidence from the *Sunna* forbidding it and this is nowhere mentioned. Some eminent and virtuous people, knowing the times and the people, their sluggishness in devotion and lack of desire for goodness, see no harm in gathering them for the remembrance of God the Exalted and introducing poetry that is sound both in its meanings and its form, for souls are attracted to it and this leads them to gather for the remembrance of God the Exalted. To each man according to his intention and God, Transcendent and Exalted is He, is the One Who sees what is hidden [within each person]. Those who think ill [of others] and harbor malice will perceive beauty as ugliness and ugliness as beauty. One should be no less than fair and do no less than refrain [from passing judgment] where things are unclear. Those who do not know the truth should seek it from its people. Everything that contradicts the Book and *Sunna* is to be rejected and everything that diverges from the pattern of the virtuous predecessors is evil, whenever the origin of the divergence is antagonism and obstinacy, for the truth is vast, the permissible is different from the superior and is not the same as the recommended, neither is the recommended the same as the obligatory. We possess clear sight in our affairs and guidance from our Lord. The Book of God and the *Sunna* of His Messenger (may blessings and peace be upon him) are with us. We are neither ignorant in religious matters, innovators, followers of those passions that lead astray, nor do we put our reason above the religion of God the Exalted. We accept the truth from whoever brings it to us, we conform to it and are not arrogant, and we do not imitate other men.

Understand the answers we have given to your questions for we have advanced no word but that we have for it unequivocal evidence from the Book of God the Exalted, the *Sunna* of His Messenger (may blessings and peace be upon him) and the words of the Imāms of guidance, but we have omitted them for the sake of brevity, for the best words are those which are brief yet informative. He whom God guides will be rightly-guided and he whom God leads astray will find no guiding patron.

It seems that you are a fanatical supporter of your school of thought, that you accept only that which conforms to it, and see no truth but there. If that is so, then speaking to you will be useless, unless you believe that your school is indeed the truth but that the truth is neither confined nor limited to it, so that you misjudge those who diverge from it as much as the span of a hand, then there is benefit in speaking to you and it is in the hope of this that we have answered you. One such benefit is that you should not believe that this region is without someone who knows the truth, is able to express it and fight those who deviate from it with his tongue, sword, lances, help and allies as much as he is able and permitted to do.

None can be criticized for being weak or neglectful who has done all that was possible and spent all his energy. Another is that you, having lived in this city for a time and having claimed that you loved it and loved its people, and now being on the verge of leaving it, should not depart harboring ill-thinking for its people or what you claim you saw them do, for they are the People of the House whom God the Exalted has purified and made it an obligation on you and all other Muslims to befriend and support. "*God guides whom He will to a straight path,*" "*my success is from no other than God, on him do I rely and to him do I return.*" "*Praised be God Who has guided us to this and we would not have been guided had He not guided us.*" "*The Messengers of our Lord have come with the truth.*" "*Transcendent are You, we have no knowledge save that which You have taught us, You are indeed the Knowing, the Wise.*" And may God bless our master Muḥammad, his family and Companions and grant them peace.

This was dictated on Monday the fourth of Jumādā al-Ūlā in the year 1073 of the Emigration of the Prophet, may the best of blessings and peace be upon him.

95

One of his companions asked him about the interpretation of His Words, Exalted is He: "*And he who turns away from My remembrance, his shall be a*

> *life of narrowness and on the Day of Resurrection We shall raise him blind. He shall say, 'O my Lord, why have You raised me blind and I used to have eyesight?' He shall say, 'So it is, Our signs came to you and you forgot them, and so today you are forgotten.'*" [20:124]

He answered: Know that commentators have differed on some of its meanings, but the differences are mostly ones of terminology.

We shall mention with the utmost brevity, God willing, what is clearer and more correct. God the Exalted has said: "*And whosoever turns away from My remembrance*," meaning from the Qur'ān and the right guidance by not believing in it, which is the state of those who disbelieve and deny; "*his shall be a life of narrowness*," in this world, because of his passionate desire for it, he will remain in distress even though to all outward appearances he is affluent or else his portion will be meager and accompanied with impatience and frustration. The Intermediary World (*Barzakh*) [will be distressful] because of the kinds of torments he will be made to endure in his grave, the narrowness of the pit, the tormenting by the angels, the attacks by injurious beasts, and so on. The Hereafter [will be even more distressful because he will be made to] eat bitter thorn-fruit and drink boiling water, perpetually subsisting in the Fire. We ask God for safety! "*And on the Day of Resurrection we shall raise him blind*." That is blind of both heart and eyesight. "*He shall say, 'O my Lord why have You raised me blind*?" Here he denies the blindness in his eyesight which is new to him while he still has blindness of the heart. "*And I used to have eyesight*," in the world. "*He shall say, 'So it is, Our signs came to you and you forgot them*,'" shunned and ignored them, "*and so today you are forgotten*," left in your blindness, wretchedness, painful torment and excessive torture. We ask God to make us and you firm in faith and guard us against deviating and straying. Praised be God in all states.

96

Another of his companions asked him about the ram that the people of al-Ghīl have a custom of leaving free to roam their houses and which they call *Musāyir*.

He answered: The ram that the people of al-Ghīl have a custom of leaving in their houses which they call *Musāyir* and which they replace with another whenever it departs is a kind of association with God (*shirk*), may God protect us! Such association is an immense injustice. It is, together with other similar things, a cause for the Devil and his troops to gain sway over those people who do such things, for God the Exalted has given the Devil sway over whoever follows him from the children of Adam, and such practices are one kind of following him. God the Exalted has said: "*Over my servants you shall have no authority except those who follow you, being perverse.*" [15:42] Do not do that and let none of the town's inhabitants who obey you do it. There is, in seeking protection in God, His Messenger, the Verses of the Qur'ān, and the performance of the ritual prayers, enough protection from the evil of all demons whether of the jinn or the humans. You have received the talisman that the Messenger of God, blessings and peace be upon him, wrote for Abū-Dujāna when he complained to him that jinn appeared in his house. When he put it in the house they fled it and retreated in haste. Hang the copy that we sent you in your house after making another copy which you can leave where it can be seen and copied for any Muslim who wants it, on condition that you abandon this *Musāyir* and rely only on God other than Whom none can benefit or harm. Had those people relied on God, purified themselves from defilement and established the ritual prayers, no demon would come near them and no jinn would harm them, on the contrary they would flee them, for the plotting of the devil is feeble.

As for sicknesses and infirmities, they are sometimes sent by God to His faithful servants that He may reward them. Much more afflictions and misfortunes may be driven toward those who carry out such practices and are attached to the jinn, however, they will be sinful and encumbered, not given their wages and rewards. So hold firmly to God and take protection in Him. Beware of testing God which is for a man to say "Read this verse, write down this talisman or take the advice of such a virtuous man, then see what happens!" To do this is to doubt and because of this most people are deprived of the blessings of the virtuous (*ṣāliḥūn*) and the blessings of their advice, so much so that they now say: "There remains in these times none of the people of secrets and *karāmāt*." They are held off by their poor determination and little sincerity and certitude. He only benefits who is determined and whose certitude is strong to the extent that it cannot even be imagined that anything can occur to him apart from what the man of God he relies on has told him.

97

The venerable *sayyid* Aḥmad ibn 'Awād Bā-Ḥusayn Bā-'Alawī asked him about what the Sufis mean by courtesy (*adab*)?

He answered: They said different things about it, the gist of which is that a man should keep to the limits imposed by his slavehood, fulfill the rights of Lordship with utmost reverence and respect, together with abandoning and divesting oneself of all claims to be doing so or to see oneself as doing it. [This is the result of] either their absorption in the perception of the Real moving them to do it or their absorption in the perception of their own shortcomings and the attributes of their souls which leaves no room for their giving themselves any consideration or importance. This is the sum of what they have said about courtesy, may God the Exalted have mercy on them.

98

> The same *sayyid* also asked him: "What should one intend when one salutes the virtuous *(ṣaliḥūn)* in his ritual prayer, and who are the virtuous meant by this salute?"

He answered: Know that virtue *(ṣalāḥ)* is an exalted degree and God the Exalted attributes it [in the Qur'ān] to a number of His Prophets. He describes Abraham, Jesus, and John (*Yaḥyā*) (may peace be upon them) with the term *ṣāliḥūn*. Reflect on the verses where this is mentioned and it should suffice you. When saluting the *ṣāliḥūn* in this context one should intend those whom the Messenger of God (may God's blessings and peace be upon him) intended when he taught his community the *Tashahhud*.

99

> He also asked him whether if he were to recite *sūra al-Sajda* and *Tabārak* in the *sunna* prayer after *'Ishā'* he would not need to recite them before going to bed.

He answered: Yes it would suffice, as has been handed down.

100

> And he asked him about whether the invocations before sleep could be recited whenever one wished to sleep and was making ready for it?

He answered: All the invocations attached to sleep whether *tasbīḥ* or otherwise can be performed when one wishes to sleep and begins to make ready for it. Some should be done only after lying down, according to what is in the *ḥadiths* concerning this matter.

101

He asked whether the *musabba'āt* could be requited later if missed.

He answered: Yes, they should be requited and they should be completed after sunrise and sunset as other time-bound invocations are.

102

He asked him about attending gatherings where audition is held using tambourines and lutes (*'ūd*).

He answered: Attending gatherings where they use tambourines and lutes in audition is dangerous unless in the presence of the perfect among gnostic men and with their permission. Try therefore to avoid that whenever possible. Talking about audition may involve much lengthy elaboration and it was fully done by our master, Imām al-Ghazālī (may God's mercy be upon him) in the *"Iḥyā'"* where he devoted a whole section to it.

103

He asked him about those who feel more inclination for the sciences of the outward than for those of the inward.

He answered: To be more inclined to sciences of the outward than those of the inward is of the enticements of the ego and insinuations of the Enemy. To use the need of the people for the outward sciences as an argument is an error for they need even more those of the inward. For one's inward to be lacking in inward knowledge detracts from one's faith (*Īmān*) while lack of outward knowledge detracts from one's *Islām*[42], they are inseparable but the first is more noble. So be eager for both, keen to acquire them, and strive to acquire both. Be more concerned and careful to acquire the more important and profitable one. Speaking of such matters needs much elaboration and were I to devote a separate work to each, they would be worthy of it. Those who possess the knowledge of God and of His religion are keeping silent because people have turned away from God and from taking His path, they lack the desire for knowledge and have no patience for seeking the truth and its people, they neither follow them nor, when they find them, do they take of what they possess. This has now become the rule and the dominant attribute of the people of this time, save those whom God guards and a very few these are.

104

He also asked him about addressing correspondence with the formula from so and so to so and so.

He answered: Your beginning your last letter with from so and so to so and so is the *Sunna* and [appropriate] courtesy, this was the way of the predecessors and their virtuous successors, so keep to it.

105

And he asked him about reciting some of his *awrād* as he walks along.

He answered: There is no harm in that and no reproach if done with the heart as present and collected as when sitting down. Thus state the superior scholars as concerns the recitation [of Qur'ān] and *awrād*.

106

The same *sayyid* also asked him about the regular recitation of the blessed and venerable litanies *(aḥzāb)* of Shaykh Abul Ḥasan al-Shādhilī (may God's mercy be on him).

He answered: Recite regularly *Ḥizb al-Barr* with the morning *awrād* and *Ḥizb al-Baḥr* after *'Aṣr*. As for Shaykh Ḥusayn Bilfaqīh's opinion concerning these, it is clear. However, one should give priority in that time to what was received from the Messenger of God (may God's blessings and peace be upon him). For example, when you wish to recite *Ḥizb al-Baḥr* after *'Aṣr*, you should recite first the *tasbīḥ*, *taḥmīd*, and *takbīr*. When the time prescribed is the same, recite the Prophetic invocations first. The rest is clear.

Your additions to our compilations of morning and evening invocations are acceptable, recite them afterwards. Read the People's books as much as you can, whether you understand or not, for in them is *baraka* and goodness.

These two litanies should suffice you from the litanies of the Shādhilīs. To learn the Prophetic invocations and supplications is better and nearer to perfection.

The unclear passages in those litanies one should neither preoccupy oneself with nor object to; one should reflect on whatever is clear and understand it. A thing is clear when it has an obvious meaning and a known context. What is unclear or problematic is what is difficult to understand.

You say you have added blessings and peace on the Messenger of God (may God's blessings and peace be upon him) and the word "Messenger" after "Prophet", in the formula beginning with "*raḍītu...*" (I am content with...), there is no harm in this. A version has been transmitted with the term "Messenger"; however, the other one is sounder. Using both is to be encouraged.

107

The venerable *sayyid* 'Abdallāh ibn 'Aqīl ibn Shaykh asked him about the meaning of some verses of poetry, the first of which was:

From every subtle meaning I drink a cup
and each speaking creature in the universe charms me.

The second:

O happiness of the eye, ask my eye if it has used the *kohl*
of a beautiful sight since you hid, O my hope!

And the third:

When you see that God is in everything the Actor
You see that everything that exists is lovely
But when you see only the appearances of His making
You are veiled and have rendered the lovely ugly.

"What is the meaning and definition of this vision and what is its reality, since God, Transcendent and Exalted is He, is beyond color, form, or personality?"

He replied: The meaning of the verses that you inquire about and that of similar verses is clear and presents no problems, for the vision is that of the heart, either through the eyes of learning and taking heed, or through the eye of experiential contemplation which is the inner eyesight, and these need no form, color, personality, face to face meeting, or any other perceivable corporeal attribute. This is how believers shall see their Lord in the Garden, although this [vision] will be through the outer eyesight. However, there the outer eyesight will be like the inner eyesight and secrets of this world.

As for the first verse it indicates that the world has become for him an intermediary governed in every way by Divine Knowledge. This does actually happen and is a sound [spiritual] state for those in it.

As for the second verse, it indicates that he sees none other than Him and whenever he looks at any other he sees in a true vision only the One who gave it its appearance and manifested it. In this there is a certain exaggeration which is acceptable from those who are in love and yearning.

As for the last two verses, if you see that God is, in everything, the Actor etc., this is to see the attribute of the Maker in the made object, to see in every act the effect of the Actor, His wisdom, His wondrous precision, the reason and purpose of His creating them, that which He wants to do with and for them; all these are good and beautiful and contain no ugliness and no imperfection. Those whose ill-fortune and bad choice it is to reverse this vision may see ugliness in all or some things. This does not include the legally approved or disapproved things, there are for these other meanings which come from a different route which is the Divine Command [i.e. Revelation].[43]

As for attributing transcendence, holiness and exaltation beyond any creature's attribute, to the Real, it is agreed upon from both the perspective of the Law and that of realization. It is such in both this world and the Hereafter, but the people of the path tend to overstep some limits and exaggerate, some may speak immoderately when overpowered [by a spiritual state], they are all excusable and there are justifications for what they say that are known by those who are qualified. Nothing is vaster than divinely related things, nothing clearer to those who are qualified, and nothing more perilous to the unqualified, especially if delved into without an authoritative shaykh to guide them along these routes and accompany them through these dominions. God guides whom He will to a straight path.

108

The venerable *sayyid* Aḥmad ibn Zayn al-Ḥabashī Bā-Alawī, the compiler of the *fatāwa,* questioned him about how one should interpret the verses and *ḥadiths* indicating that the torment of the disbelievers, may God protect us from it, is permanent and

> endless knowing that Imām Aḥmad has transmitted on the authority of ibn 'Umar that, "There shall come a day when the gates of *Jahannam* will be clapping and there will remain no one in it," and that following their spending long periods in it. Many others have transmitted similar [traditions] from ibn Mas'ūd and Abū Hurayra, and ibn Taymiya related it on the authority of other Companions.

He answered: You ask about something about which too much has already been said. Some scholars among the People of *Sunna* have objected to certain people belonging to the Path of God who have accepted the *ḥadith* that you have quoted and said that the torments of the people of the Fire, the idolaters and disbelievers, will come to an end. They have no compelling proof in this *ḥadith*, even supposing it to be authentic, for the numerous texts from the Book and *Sunna* that have reached the level of *tawātur* and are not open to interpretation cannot be countered with such illusions. A certain scholar, having quoted both points of view, then proposed an explanation combining them. He said: "The Fire has seven tiers the highest of which is called *Jahannam*, this is the place of the sinners among the believers and there is no doubt that their faith will bring them out of it, each in his own time, and, once they all depart, it will be left vacant." That is reasonable enough, but I still do not accept it because it does not solve the problem. There is no alternative here but to accept the textual evidence of the Book and *Sunna* and that which both our early predecessors and their successors in this community have agreed upon.

Know that whoever reads widely in different sciences will come across many similar matters which may arouse some illusions and problems [in his mind] and an enlightened intellect and a sound mind will rescue him from these.

The one who accepts a comprehensive statement of beliefs that has the approval of the majority of the People of *Sunna* will have protected his belief.

We have come across many such things in books and God has protected us from being deluded by them or pursuing whatever was ambiguous. We are aware in that matter which you have raised and other similar ones of many long discourses by many sufis, I think Shaykh ibn Ḥajar has alluded to that question somewhere in "*al-Zawājir*" but it is long since I have last read this book. Nothing is problematic for "*Whoever has a heart or listens with attentiveness.*"

109

> The Sufi scholar Shaykh 'Abdallāh ibn Sa'īd ibn 'Uthmān al-'Amūdī asked him about his opinion concerning those who were never reached by the summons [to Islam] but who nevertheless behaved in certain matters according to the religious Law, having been guided to them by God; would they be rewarded with the Garden and become like its people?

He answered: Regarding your question, know first of all that scholars of authority in these matters have disagreed on those who lived in the periods between [each two consecutive] Prophets as well as those who live in remote areas of the vast earth and were thus never reached by the summons [to Islam]. Some held that they would be punished since they were not believers in the oneness of God and God does not forgive those who associate others with Him. Others held that they would not be punished since the summons never reached them and there is therefore no case against them; and God the Exalted says in many verses: "*We never chastise, until We send forth a Messenger.*" Others still held that one should refrain [from formulating an opinion], which is the safer and wiser course since the evidence for each opinion, whether textual or rational, seems to all outward appearances to be somewhat contradictory, although the reality of the matter is that no contradiction at all exists. As for someone who, as you mention, was not reached by the Messenger but, as a gift from God to him and a guidance that God the Exalted favored him with, believed and performed the kinds of devotions that were made lawful through the Messenger (may blessings and peace be upon him), and this is not impossible although we have never heard of it happening. If then we assume that it is possible, his state would be far better than those who were never reached by the Messenger but neither believed nor acted according to the Law. It has been said that he would be treated mercifully and spared all torment. Among those who are of this opinion is the Imām, the Proof of Islam, in his book "The Difference Between Disbelief and Heresy." God knows best the reality of things, their consequences, where they will come to rest, and of all things [He knows] all possible detail from all possible angles. The one who studies these things, if he is one who fears God and guards himself [against His wrath], can never speak definitively or conclusively except with regards to what is explicitly stated in *sharī'a* and specifically mentioned unequivocally and in the absence of any other statement which may contradict it. In such matters this is almost impossible. So do reflect on what we have said, it is comprehensive and contains more than the question involved. God it is who guides to the truth.

110

The same *Sayyid* Aḥmad asked him whether a man affiliated to a shaykh of the Path can increase in rank through his shaykh without being aware of it? If that is so, then what is the reason, is it his love for his shaykh and his Path, or his attraction to his pat-

> tern of behavior and his perceiving him as perfect? And if this is so, can it be strengthened and increased?

He answered: Yes, he is improved by [the shaykh's solicitous] gaze and his own reverence and good opinion of him, and he becomes aware of certain parts of that increase but not of others. He increases and benefits more from this than from his own strivings and deeds. However, when both are joined in the disciple he becomes more worthy of increase and more likely to benefit. As for that which strengthens the things that we have just mentioned, it is for the disciple to dwell on the virtuous deeds and pleasing behavior that reinforce his belief in the shaykh and reverence for him. On the whole, there is nothing more profitable to the disciple than to lose himself in the shaykh and think well and believe in him to perfection. With these, a little concentration and striving is worth much and vice versa. To explain this question in detail would be lengthy, we have mentioned some of this in the "Book of the Disciple", reflect on it and, God willing, it will suffice you.

111

> The *sayyid* 'Abdallāh ibn Muḥammad Musāwā asked him about the teaching of children and others, as well as about many other things.

He answered: Teaching children as well as others is required and encouraged by Law on condition that one possesses the knowledge and has sincerity with God the Exalted. Knowledge here means to teach what you know and keep silent about what you do not know, for God does not like those who pretend, and the sin of the one who speaks of what he does not know is greater than that of the one who speaks not what he knows. As for reading the books of Ghazālī, you say that you have read some and that our book, "*al-Naṣā'iḥ*", should be sufficient. Know that that is partly so, but in the books of Ghazali there is light, blessing, benefit and secrets. They have an effect which no other [book] has. So do read them, together with "*al-Naṣā'iḥ*" as much as you can, either the "*Iḥyā'*", the "*al-Arbe'īn al-Aṣl*", or "*Minhājul 'Ābidīn.*" May God take over your guidance, take hold of our heart and yours and lead them to what He likes and is pleased with, with good endings; Amen!

As for marriage, there is no harm in it. There are in it gains and profits as well as responsibilities and hindrances. So weigh each against the other and be where the balance weighs heavier. As regards choosing from the *sharīfs* or from others, know that concordance in kind is better, purer and more suitable. Whatever God has decreed and ordained, that is good provided there is nothing frivolous in it, either in the eyes of *Sharī'a* or common custom.

112–118

The Sufi Shaykh 'Abdallāh ibn Sa'īd al-'Amudī asked him about the definition of sincerity (*ṣidq*), the sincere (*ṣādiq*), total truthfulness (*ṣiddīqiyya*) and the *ṣiddīq*, as well as about other things.

112

He answered: As for your question about the definition of *ṣidq* and *ṣādiq*, know that *ṣidq* is a noble state and the term is used to indicate that both one's inward and outward are united in the effort to achieve the desired goal in the appropriate and most complete manner. The *ṣādiq* is he who is established in this state and there is of necessity differences in degree between such people, some being more complete than others. The maximum of the *ṣādiq* is to reach the beginning of the degrees of *ṣiddīqiyya*.

113

As for your question about the definition of the *ṣiddīqiyya* and the *ṣiddīq*, the *ṣiddīq* is the one who has acquired all the degrees of *ṣidq* and states of the *ṣādiq* in the fullest and firmest way, free from doubts or changes. The *ṣiddīq* is the one in whom this description is established and who is firmly stationed in this degree. He is the believer who is perfect in faith, certitude, concentration on drawing near to God the Exalted, acting for the sake of God, and summoning others to Him by both his state and his words. The people of this degree differ, some are more perfect than others, the upper limit of *ṣiddīqiyya* is Prophethood (*nubuwwa*).

Is there another degree between Prophethood and *ṣiddīqiyya*? There are differences of opinion. The gnostic Shaykh Muḥyiddīn ibn 'Arabī, the author of the "*Futūḥāt*", mentioned that between them was another degree termed the Degree of Nearness (*Qurba*) and he wrote on that a pleasant work which we came across; it was read to us in Ta'iz of Yemen by a man of knowledge and Sufism called Yūsuf al-Jāwī (the Javanese) who is one of our companions.

We hold that there is no separate degree or station between Prophethood and *ṣiddīqiyya* and that this Nearness (*Qurba*) that ibn 'Arabī (may God's mercy be upon him) spoke about is the highest station [within *ṣiddīqiyya*]. It is a special attribute of some of the people in this noble degree just as Friendship (*Khilla*), Conversation (*Kalām*), Spirituality (*Rūḥiyya*)[44], and other similar matters [are attributes] in the stations of Prophethood and Messengership special to some of the people of this sublime and noble degree. And God gave them all to our Prophet, (may blessings and peace be upon him), thus giving him supremacy over all other Prophets and Messengers. Shaykh ibn 'Arabī says that in this degree of Nearness is al-Khidr, for he is above the *ṣiddīqiyya* but below the Prophets, as are those whose states are similar to his such as Dhul-Qarnayn[45] and Mary (may peace be upon them). We hold that the truth in this matter is what we have mentioned and this will be evident for those who think about it in the writings of the Proof of Islam and other authorities. He (al-Ghazālī) mentions it in "*al-Arbe'īn al-Aṣl*" and other works. Shaykh ibn 'Arabī made a reference to what the Proof of Islam had written, then said: "This degree, meaning that of nearness, may remain hidden from even some of the greatest authorities such as Imām al-Ghazālī, for he never mentioned a degree between *Ṣiddīqiyya* and Prophethood." That is what we see and God knows best.

114

You ask about Mastery (*Tamkīn*) and whether it applies to all stations. Yes, it does apply to each one of them. A servant may have mastery in some but not all stations. For example, he may have mastery in the stations of sincerity (*ikhlās*) and renunciation (*zuhd*), but not in those of reliance (*tawakkul*) and love (*maḥabba*). The one who is given the mastery of all stations is the one who is truly masterful.

Mastery is complete stability and firm establishment in a station so that the possessor of that station never wavers and never changes, he is not overcome by spiritual states, nor is he swayed by them. This may be specific to one state or general, including them all, as we mentioned before.

115

As for your question about the lowest and highest [degrees of] certitude of the *ṣādiq* and the lowest and highest [degrees of] certitude of the *ṣiddīq*, this is a question that cannot very well be asked since both the *ṣādiq* and the *ṣiddīq* are people of complete certitude. The very most that one can say is that the certitude of the *ṣiddīq* is more complete than that of the *ṣādiq* and that the *ṣādiqūn* differ in their [degree of] certitude according to the differences between their [degrees] of *ṣidq*, and so do the *ṣiddīqūn*.

One may ask about the lowest and highest [degrees of] certitude only where the generality of believers are concerned. We have alluded to that at the beginning of the "Book of Assistance" so look it up there. It is to the certitude of the *ṣiddīqūn* that the Commander of the Faithful, 'Alī ibn Abī Ṭālib (may God be pleased with him) was referring when he said: "Were the cover to be removed I would not increase in certitude." The cover is inevitable in this abode, it is a veil which may become so thin and subtle that some people of [direct] vision may think that neither cover nor veil remains, but the truth is that a veil is inescapable as long as a human being is in this abode. Even if it be reduced to only the physical body and human form of the man of vision, it is still a veil for him.

116

As for your question about whether in the stations of *ṣiddīqiyya,* all or some of them, there is pleasure for the soul in all or some of its stations: Yes, there is pleasure and delight in it but it is not termed a passion since when the soul has the noble attribute and the high rank that *ṣiddīqiyya* is, it can be but a serene soul, in whom all human passions and all physical appetites have been extinguished. Felicity of the soul lies in this [spiritual rank], comes from and is caused by it. This felicity resembles that of the people in the Garden in that it neither distracts nor veils them from God, provided they are of those whose attribute is extinction (*fanā'*) and subsistence (*baqā'*). Think about the fullness of these meanings in the words of ibn 'Aṭā'illāh towards the end of the "*Ḥikam*", where he says: "...should they descend to the heaven of obligations or the earth of allotted shares," etc.[46]

117

As for your question about whether the *Afrād* are outside the circle of the *Quṭb*, the *Ghawth*, as some have said, know that we were asked about this matter a long time ago and answered it as sufficed for the time and place. We now say: God has in His creation hidden secrets, particularities, and ways of disposing of things which only He knows fully. Those who are given some of the secrets, shown a hidden thing, or given power of action over part of His Kingdom, live according to what He gave them. They may think in a limitative manner and reckon that beyond that nothing else exists, or be open and know that what they have is but a little out of plenty, a small portion of something immense, and that "*they will only encompass of His knowledge that which He will.*" "*Of knowledge you have been given but a little.*" The *Quṭb* and *Ghawth* is the leader of the Saints of the Circle, the people who dispose of things. They are the ones whose numbers were given in *those ḥadiths* that relate to them. If God should reveal to a servant of His that He has saints who appear to be other than those numbered ones, they may still belong to them but he may have been shown some of their subtle secret realities that are unrelated to the Circles or to the [function of] disposing. He may then mistake them for men when they are, [in reality] subtle realities of some of the men of the Circles. If his vision of them is sound and they are in effect men, then we will accept it from him if he is one [whose degree makes him] worthy of it, for the things of God are formidable, His Kingdom vast, and His secrets innumerable, as we have said before. But we do not accept it from every one who is of that nature [i.e., a man of vision] unless we know that he has the station which encompasses all stations and that he is the Perfect Man (*al-Insān al-Kāmil*) or someone close to this station such as the two *Imāms*, the four *Awtād* or the seven *Abdāl*. As for people of the path who may have some direct perception (*dhawq*) and mastery, they may see things and utter words which the people of [outward] authority will consider false and excessive when they are, for them, true. They are excusable on account of their being overcome by their states and the Divine things which are unbearable and with which they can but say what they say. These may be the words that were reported to have been said by the Sufi Shaykh Aḥmad Bā-'Abdal-Qādir, if he is indeed the one to have said them and none has said them before, and if he has related them about someone else then the person who said them is of such kind (may God have mercy on them). "*God says the truth and it is He who guides along the way.*"

You mentioned in a recent letter what you understood from a letter of ours where we mentioned that the men of God may generally be divided into three categories and that opposite each category there is one kind of deceitful people who parody the truthful but are far removed from truth and its people. Both what you and your friend have understood is acceptable. However, the liar who is the counterpart of the truthful is in reality in a state which is the opposite of his. The two may be confused, as far as appearances are concerned, only by those who have no firm knowledge and no insight "*that that which God has decreed may come to pass.*"

As for what you said about extinction (*fanā'*) and subsistence (*baqā'*), know that only to experience these and realize them in oneself and not simply be informed about them is of any consequence. One can learn about the states of extinction and subsistence while being neither a man of extinction nor one of subsistence and can thus claim for himself something that is not his because he is unable to distinguish between those matters which he is able to learn about and those which he should experience.

Your question: "Is extinction one of existence (*wujūd*) or witnessing (*shuhūd*), and similarly for subsistence?" Know that the matter is complex. In some situations it is an extinction of existence and in others an extinction of witnessing only, while existence remains as it is. In most cases extinction involves both the existence and the witnessing of attributes but not of the bodies. The same applies to subsistence. The extinct man may be extinct to existence while existence remains as it is; he is only extinct to his actions and perception of it. There are many details [that need to be mentioned here] and need lengthy elaboration, so think deeply about what we have said, reflect well on it and the meaning will appear to you, even if gradually.

118

You mentioned in your previous letter that you were writing a book and intended to mention in one of its chapters those whom you have taken from. When you came to visit and showed it to us, you had proceeded to the point where you mention us. If your intention is to mention in that chapter of the work those whom you have taken from, then, God willing, this is appropriate. And if your intention is that we mention to you some of those from whom we have taken and some of our chains of transmission as far as the *khirqa* and other such matters are concerned, then know that we have met and taken from numerous people, both of the Bā-'Alawī *sayyids* and others whom we have known in Tarīm, other parts of Hadramawt, or have met in our journeys to the two honorable Sanctuaries for *Ḥajj* and to Yemen. These are so numerous that to enumerate them would be too lengthy; were we to do so they would perhaps number more than one hundred scholars, gnostics, and virtuous brothers. We were once asked to enumerate them and relate some of their merits but were prevented from doing so by some of the time's events, the lack of interest of its people for such matters and other hindrances. Not every hindrance can be mentioned, as Imām Mālik ibn Anas (may God have mercy on him) has said. We shall however mention a few of them in a summary way.

Know that we have taken outward knowledge from a number of its people and studied it thoroughly in appropriate times. Then we took the sciences of the Path from a number of its people, some well known and others whose state was hidden. They were, in that time, the remaining ones[47] and they have departed to God the Exalted and the Last Abode. One of the most venerable of the people of the Path was the Sufi *sayyid* the *Malāmatī*[48] 'Aqīl ibn 'Abdal-Raḥmān ibn Muḥammad ibn 'Aqīl al-Saqqāf Bā-'Alawī. We visited him frequently, took from him, and were invested with the *khirqa* by him. He told me when investing me that he had never invested anyone else. We also met the exemplary *sayyid*, the comprehensive scholar Abu-Bakr, son of the exemplary *sayyid* 'Abdal-Raḥmān ibn Shihāb, the Sufi *sayyid*, 'Abdal-Raḥmān ibn Shaykh Mawlā-'Aydīd Bā-'Alawī and his son the *majdhūb* gnostic *sayyid* 'Umar ibn Aḥmad al-Hadī ibn Shihāb Bā-'Alawī, the *Majdhūb Malāmatī sayyid*, Sahl ibn Muḥammad Bā-Ḥasan al-Ḥadilī Bā-'Alawī, the superior authoritative *sayyid* Shaykh 'Umar ibn 'Abdal-Raḥmān al-'Aṭṭās who lived in Ḥurayḍa and whom we met many times and from whom we took the complete manner of *dhikr*, *muṣāfaḥa*[49], and investiture with the *khirqa*. We also took from the illustrious and celebrated gnostic *sayyid* Shaykh Muḥammad ibn 'Alawī Bā-'Alawī who lived in Makka the Honorable through written letters but we never met him physically. He also invested us by correspondence, May God have mercy on them all, make us benefit from them and give us and all Muslims of their blessings and secrets. As for the chains of transmission we shall mention something of them. We shall start with the chain of transmission of *sayyid* Muḥammad ibn 'Alawī and say: We took the investiture of the *khirqa* from *sayyid* Muḥammad ibn 'Alawī and he gave us authorization (*ijāza*) for it. And from the gnostic *sayyid* Shaykh 'Abdallāh ibn 'Alī of al-Waḥṭ[50] who took from the two venerable authoritative shaykhs *sayyid* Shaykh ibn 'Abdallāh al-'Aydarūs, the author of "*al-'Iqd al-Nabawī*" and *sayyid* 'Umar ibn 'Abdallāh al-'Aydarūs who is buried in Aden. *Sayyid* Shaykh was invested by his father *sayyid* 'Abdallāh ibn Shaykh who took from his paternal uncle the illustrious Pole, Shaykh Abū-Bakr son of the master Shaykh 'Abdallāh ibn Abu-Bakr al-'Aydarūs. *Sayyid* 'Umar took from his father, *sayyid* 'Abdallāh, who took from his father *sayyid* 'Alawī son of the Shaykh 'Abdallāh al-'Aydarūs. *Sayyid* 'Alawī took from his brother the Pole, the Shaykh, the *sayyid* Abū-Bakr ibn 'Abdallāh of Aden. Thus the chain of transmission of *sayyid* Shaykh and *sayyid* 'Umar were joined in Shaykh Abū-Bakr. As for the gnostic shaykh *sayyid* 'Umar ibn 'Abdal-Raḥmān al-'Aṭṭās, he took from the Shaykh *sayyid* al-Ḥusayn son of the authoritative Shaykh, the Pole Abū-Bakr ibn Sālim. Shaykh al-Ḥusayn took from his father Shaykh Abū-Bakr who took from the Shaykh *sayyid* 'Umar ibn Muḥammad Bā-Shaybān. As we were informed, Shaykh 'Umar Bā-Shaybān took from the Shaykh, the exemplar, *sayyid* 'Abdal-Raḥmān son of the comprehensive Imām Shaykh 'Alī ibn Abū-Bakr. Shaykh 'Abdal-Raḥmān took from his father, the said Shaykh 'Alī ibn Abū-Bakr. As for the Sufi *sayyid* 'Aqīl ibn 'Abdal-Raḥmān, whom we mentioned before, he took from his father, the gnostic *sayyid* 'Abdal-Raḥmān ibn Muḥammad ibn 'Aqīl, who took from the gnostic *sayyid*, the unique man of his time, Shaykh Aḥmad ibn 'Alawī Bā-Jaḥdab, who took from the aforementioned *sayyid* 'Umar ibn Muḥammad Bā-Shaybān.

As for our master Shaykh Abū-Bakr ibn 'Abdallāh al-'Aydarūs of Aden, he took from his father, the Pole of the gnostics, 'Abdallāh ibn Abū-Bakr and from his paternal uncle, the authoritative Shaykh 'Alī ibn Abū-Bakr. Those two shaykhs took from their father al-Sakrān Abū-Bakr son of the Shaykh, the master, 'Abdal-Raḥmān al-Saqqāf and their paternal uncle the comprehensive Shaykh 'Umar al-Meḥḍār son of Shaykh 'Abdal-Raḥmān.

As for *sayyid* 'Umar ibn Muḥammad Bā-Shaybān, we have said before that he took from Shaykh 'Abdal-Raḥmān son of Shaykh 'Alī, Shaykh 'Abdal-Raḥmān took from his father Shaykh 'Alī and his paternal uncle Shaykh 'Abdallāh ibn Abū-Bakr al-'Aydarūs, whom we mentioned before among those we took from.

If you wish to complete those chains of transmission look into "*al-Barqa*", the book of our master the Shaykh, the master 'Alī ibn Abū-Bakr. It is a book he wrote about the investiture of the *khirqa* and those from whom he took this Path. Look also into the "Noble Volume" (*al-Juz' al-Sharīf*) written by our master the Shaykh, the Pole Abū-Bakr ibn 'Abdallāh al-'Aydarūs concerning those he took from, and their chains of transmission, and join that to what we have mentioned. You may write briefly if you wish or in detail, for there is room here for elaboration or details since these are numerous *khirqas*.

There are many chains of transmission going back to our master the greatest teacher, the foremost scholar (*al-Faqīh al-Muqaddam*) Muḥammad ibn 'Alī 'Alawī to our master the revered master, Shaykh Muḥiyyidīn 'Abdal-Qādir Abū Ṣāliḥ al-Jīlī, and to many other shaykhs mentioned in the two works we have named, the "*Barqa*" of our master Shaykh 'Alī ibn Abū-Bakr and "*al-Juz' al-Sharīf*" of our master Shaykh Abū-Bakr ibn 'Abdallāh al-'Aydarūs. If you want those two books then look for them; you may find them where you are in Daw'an, otherwise write to us and we shall send them to you. May God the Exalted lead us to all kinds of good, reform our intentions, aims, inwards and outwards, and give us, you, our friends, and all Muslims to conclude our lives in virtue and goodness.

119

The same man also said: "If a man of tasting (*dhawq*) and contemplation (*shuhūd*) says that 'opposites unite in a single state in the vision of unification,' is it correct to say to him: 'Yes, on condition that the Law (*sharī'a*) is given its due and reality (*ḥaqīqa*) its due, that reason is used to judge matters that fall under its jurisdiction, while handed down knowledge [of *sharī'a*] is used for matters that necessitate it.'?"

He answered: As for the question as posed and its answer, the question is pertinent and the answer correct except for that part of the answer which says that one should use reason to judge matters which are amenable to rational thinking, for there is nothing here of any validity. As for his saying: "by handed down knowledge," it is [already] included in his saying: "that you give the Law its due," for the Law is what has been handed down, and reality is the consequence of knowing it and behaving according to the legal pattern that those people follow who have arrived after their traveling, and God knows best.

120

The superior scholar 'Abdallāh ibn 'Uthmān al-'Amūdī asked him about Shaykh al-Akhḍar being quoted in the conclusion of the book written on the merits of the venerable shaykh Ma'rūf Bā-Jammāl, as saying to his disciple the Sufi scholar 'Umar ibn 'Abdallāh Bā-Makhrama: "I have given you authorization for sciences that neither Messenger, Prophet nor near angel knows about," etc.

He answered: Know that the meaning within these words is correct and presents no problem, but its outward form is offensive and to be disapproved of. Many things are such and one needs first of all to know that they are indeed to be attributed to those reported to have said them. If this is done, then one needs to reflect on the problematic aspect of it when there is necessity to do so. You are aware of what God, Eminent and Majestic is He, has related in His Book of the story of Moses and al-Khidr. Moses is undoubtedly firmer and superior to al-Khidr (may peace be upon them), both according to the majority who hold that al-Khidr is a saint and the others who say he is a Prophet. Nevertheless, al-Khidr knew of sciences that Moses (may peace be upon him) knew not, and this did not make him superior or preferable to Moses. That should be enough evidence for you. Degrees and stations are different from sciences and gnoses. You are aware that a particular servant of a king of this world may be informed by the king of certain secrets that he has kept from another servant who may be higher in the king's esteem and consideration from the one he has told. This happens frequently, it has its necessity, conditions and secrets. Reflect again on what you have told us and what we have said and things will become clear to you. A similar thing may happen with the children, friends or servants of a man. He may inform one of them of some of his secrets when others are higher in his esteem and consideration than the one he has informed of this particular matter. So make this your guideline and manner of solving this and similar problems in similar situations. The one who reads books comes across many such things, may God guide you. Peace be on you.

121

Al-'Amūdī also inquired about things which will become clear from the answer.

He answered: You mention the discussion that took place between some of your companions about verses of our poem, the "*Tā'iyya*", where certitude is mentioned. This matter is clear to its people and evident to them with the least amount of reflection. The author says: "Make your certainty sound for it is the foundation," etc. This refers to the Knowledge of Certainty, the Eye of Certainty, and the Truth of Certainty, and these are terms commonly employed by the People and mentioned in the Qushayrī Treatise and other works. The author also says: "...that from the soundness of the Knowledge of Certainty derives the soundness of the realities of *Islam*, from the soundness of the Eye of Certainty derives the soundness of the realities of *Imān* and from the soundness of the Truth of Certainty derives the soundness of the realities of *Iḥsān*." As for the nine stations of certainty, they are mentioned [in the passage] between his saying: "Begin by making your repentance sound," up to: "With the contentment that is appropriate to each state." These are the nine stations termed the Stations of Certainty. Shaykh Abū-Ṭālib al-Makkī explained them at great length in his book "*Qūt al-Qulūb*" and so did Imām al-Ghazālī in the volume on "Saving Things", where he explains other things as well. We mention them at the end of the "Book of Assistance" and explain them briefly and also at the end of "*al-Naṣā'iḥ*" together with the other consequences of certainty.

As for your second letter saying that you found difficulty in understanding some of the letter sent from the gnostic Shaykh 'Abdal-Raḥmān Bā-Hurmuz to his companion, the scholar Umar, there are no problems in it and nothing confusing. That which you mention you thought problematic presents no problem in any way to anyone who knows [the difference between] summary and detailed [manners of expression] and can distinguish between conditional and absolute matters, even if not expressly brought to his attention every time they are mentioned. He should use in this what he knows of the rules of every science and [be aware] that some of them are total and some partial. Know then, that it is possible that God may show a man who is not the most superior some of His secrets which He does not show others who are better; this is correct and does actually occur. This does not annul the general statements that you quoted, for what is possible is different from what is actually happening. Furthermore, that which happens in particular instances does not change the general rule. The story of al-Khidr with Moses (may peace be upon them) is sufficient to prove it, for Moses is superior to al-Khidr, but the latter was given by God knowledge of some of His secrets which He did not give to Moses, and he was informed by Him, Exalted is He, that he [al-Khidr] had more knowledge than him [Moses], meaning as far as those secrets were concerned. Now concerning the fact that nothing reaches the people of the Circle except with the knowledge of the Pole (*Quṭb*), this is correct, I mean as regards general secrets and what relates to the functions they were entrusted with for the good of the world. Similarly the saying of the Pole quoted by you: "If [as much as] an atom moves..." is a conditional matter, for this does not apply in an unrestricted and permanent way except to God, who is One and has no partners. So, if ever you hear, of what they say, similar things, know that they are conditional and particular, even if they who say them do not explicitly state so, one should know their limitations [or conditions] from the rules and principles that should be depended on. There are many examples of this even in the Book and *Sunna*, where conditional things are stated in an unrestricted manner and vice versa. This does not confuse those who are firmly established and certain of their knowledge but confuses some weak people who then stray and lose the even path.

As for your saying that the Pole's contemplative station is that of the Presence of the Name 'Allāh' and he is therefore called 'Abdallāh, etc., this was mentioned by Shaykh ibn 'Arabī with lengthy elaborations. It is correct as far as he is concerned and we concede that to him, but this statement is limiting and too narrowly specific and some of it is problematic. The summation of this is that looking into the realities and subtleties of the sciences of the People of the Path should be allowed only to those who are proficient in the exoteric sciences, have first mastered them, then disciplined their souls and refined them to perfection, then were taken by a Divine pull from Him that annihilated the remainder of their human nature, a thing that cannot be reached by discipline [or asceticism]. Otherwise, those who continuously look into the subtleties of these sciences, while not in the state of perfection that we have just described, will emerge from one problem only to fall into the next. They may become perplexed and unable to decide what to do and they may be subject to other things of a more difficult nature. So look only into those parts of their sciences that are clear. If you find a problem in them, think about it again and measure it by the rules and principles and you will know whether it is conditional or unrestricted, general or particular, total or partial, occurring continuously or only in some circumstances. And when we mention something to you, do not object to it because of what seems problematic to you and say: "They have said this and that." I am more aware and knowledgeable of what they said than you are. Take a firm hold of what we have said and reflect on it as it deserves. May God open for us and you the sight of the inner eye and guide us to what He knows is the truth in all matters, whether these are subject to differences or not, for He knows and has power over all things and knowledge of all things.

122

> He was asked about the saying of Shaykh Ḥusayn ibn 'Abdallāh Bā-Faḍl: "Take a brief *wird* to be used alone if necessary, a medium one to use when needed, and a long one to use when one's state is one of breast expansion. The briefest possible form is to silently run it in one's mind."

He answered: Praise is for God. You inquire about the saying of the Sufi Shaykh Ḥusayn son of the scholar, the Imām 'Abdallāh Balḥāj Bā-Faḍl, may God's mercy be on him, concerning *awrād* and so on. The intention and gist of it is that one should always persevere in his *awrād* and maintain them as much as possible and in a manner to suit each circumstance.

As for his saying that you should have a concise *wird*, a medium and a lengthy one:

> These differ with circumstances such as occupation or freedom, health or sickness. An example of this is what Imām al-Ghazālī mentions in "*Bidāyat al Hidāya*" to be recited before sunrise, he mentions ten invocations [formulae] to be included in the *awrād* then adds that each should be recited either one hundred, seventy, or ten times at the very least. He also mentioned them in the "*Iḥyā'*" and says: "or he can recite them three times each." This variability is due to the variability in time, energy and freedom. This also applies to the invocations mentioned in the *Sunna* to follow each ritual prayer, in the morning, evening, at bedtime, and so on. One can make these lengthy, medium or concise if he has wide knowledge of the *Sunna*. The least is to run them silently in one's mind whenever occupied with pressing matters or overpowered by an illness; which is similar to what is said about the ritual prayer of those overpowered by illness. The Shaykh intended nothing more than encouraging the disciple to take care of his *awrād* in every possible way.

123

You also ask about donating the reward for one's actions to the dead, whether one's parents, relatives or others. Know that dedicating to them the reward for charity capable of being valued in terms of money such as water, food, or any other similar thing is something that has been related in sound transmissions, and so is asking forgiveness and praying for them. God allows them to benefit from that and, by the grace of God, light, joy and other kinds of rewards do reach them. As for reciting the Qur'ān and dedicating the reward to them, scholars have differed in whether the reward reaches them, many concluding that it does and that they do benefit from it, they quote [in support] many traditions and true dreams. But transmissions concerning this are all weak. If that is so with Qur'ānic recitations, it is even more so with things like ritual prayers and fasts. Therefore one should give charity on behalf of the dead, ask for forgiveness, make *du'ā'* and ask for mercy for them. One should give some of the rewards of his charity to his parents and other such people and keep much, if not most of it to himself. Scholars have said much about this matter. Many other matters branch off from it, but this is the gist of what has been said.

124

As for your question about the words of the venerable preacher ibn Nubāta: "May God increase our reward for the affliction of prolonged distraction," I do not think that they can be justified, for being afflicted with distraction (*ghafla*) can sometimes be sinful and, rather than being disregarded, be liable of punishment. So how can one be rewarded and paid off for it? The words of the preacher (may God's mercy be on him) in many parts of his sermons are problematic, especially at the beginning of the sermons. This often occurs in the utterances of scholars, for one is human and prone to be mistaken at times and correct at others. Words may be insufficient at times, especially for expressing obscure and subtle things. The afflictions that a servant is rewarded for are those which strike him in himself, wealth and relatives, whether these be sicknesses, poverty, death or diminution, provided he remains patient in expectation of the hereafter. On the other hand, afflictions that strike one's religion are mostly sins for which a man is punished and detested, for they mostly occur by the servant's will and choice. Were the worldly afflictions to befall him by his own wish and choice he would be punishable for them. An example of this is if he injures himself or his child by his own choice, or damages his wealth, these would be punishable sins. The term affliction may be applied to both those affecting worldly and religious matters. Reward is where they affect worldly matters, not by the servant's choice, and provided he patiently endures them for the sake of God and in expectation of His reward. As for God the Exalted saying: "*Whatever good befalls you is from God and whatever evil befalls you is from yourself.*" [4:79], you quote this as evidence in your question. However, God says this concerning certain people with whose utterances He was displeased. Commentators have said that the good intended here was in the nature of fertility [of the soil] or victory [in battle] and the evil the opposite of them, bareness and defeat. Similar are His words, Exalted is He: "*If good befalls you, it vexes them; but if evil afflicts you, they rejoice at it.*" [3:120] "*If good befalls you, it vexes them; but if an affliction befalls you, they say, 'we took our dispositions before;' and turn away, rejoicing.*" [9:50] and other verses of similar meanings. As for His saying, August and Majestic is He: "*Whatever good befalls you is from God and whatever evil befalls you is from yourself.*" Scholars have given answers for it and one of the best is that between the two verses is an omitted sentence meaning: "Why do those people understand almost nothing that is said and say: 'Whatever good befalls you is from God'," etc. Meanings which are unstated or implicit are well known [to be frequent] in the Qur'ān. This concludes the answer. God it is who guides to the truth and what is right; God has more knowledge and wisdom. Think and ponder on this answer for it is comprehensive and most sufficient even though short and concise. The best of words are those that are brief yet informative.

125

The superior Shaykh Idrīs ibn Aḥmad ibn Idrīs al-Sā'dī of Makka, known as al-Shammā' asked him about the faith of the follower (*muqallid*).

He answered: As for your question concerning the science of belief and principles, know that the faith of the follower[51], as we believe and declare, is sound and undoubtedly so. This faith is to be achieved by acquisition of the knowledge and awareness of how this religion was when it was just beginning[52] and what he (may blessings and peace be upon him) accepted from the boorish among the Arabs and the desert dwellers[53], this is a clear, evident matter. As for you and those like you, we do not consider you a follower but a man of insight whose breast was expanded by God to receive faith and Islam. We hold that whoever reads the Qur'ān and understands it, even partially, and has certainty and belief in its contents, is a believer of insight. For the Qur'ān is definitely *mutawātir*[54] and definitely miraculous, and that has been so from the time of the Messenger of God (may blessings and peace be upon him) until today. How can one be a follower whose faith is the result of knowledge which is sound and proved by *tawātur* and was never denied or disputed, when faith growing out of insight may be sound even without such knowledge?

As to what al-Sanūsī has said, that is another matter. The man is a scholar of theology (*kalām*) and a strong partisan of it, and the words of any man are capable of being accepted in part and rejected in part, except those of the Messenger of God (may blessings and peace be upon him), so the Imāms have stated. If you wish to study some of the science of theology (*kalām*) do not go further than the volume on the principles of beliefs; which is in the second volume of the "*Iḥyā*'", and give more care to studying the first chapter and the third which is "*al-Risāla Al-Qudsia*". If you find in it an increase in serenity and expansion of the breast, so be it, otherwise leave it and try studying other books. The science of *kalām* is a remedy for people who have doubts and harbor suspicions, they are to take from it according to their ailment and, once cured, there is no longer much benefit or profit in studying it. That which God mentions in the Qur'ān concerning this is completely sufficient and provides the fullest benefit and profit. You will find there nothing but generalizations; the same applies to the *Sunna* and the words of the virtuous predecessors. It is to be deduced that generalizations are more beneficial than detailed expositions in this science, except for those who have doubts and problems. Imām al-Ghazālī elaborates in the volume on "Principles of Beliefs" on what we have summarized here, so study it according to your need, otherwise, if beliefs are sound in the manner that we have stated, then it is more important to occupy oneself with the sciences of the Book and *Sunna* and reforming one's heart and behavior. What we said here is a summation which you may analyze in your mind. Be thorough when you think and reflect on it! May God the Exalted guide you and us, and reinforce you and us with a spirit from Him! Amen!

126

The illumined Shaykh 'Abdallāh ibn Sa'īd al-'Amūdī asked him which is better, *ma'rifa*[55] or love?

He answered: You inquire whether knowledge (*ma'rifa*) is superior to love or vice-versa. We hold that *ma'rifa* implies more knowledge and is more incumbent, whereas love is nobler and subtler. As you have said, love is a branch of knowledge and one of its consequences. You cannot love whom you do not know, but you can know whom you do not love. We shall stop short of preferring one to the other, for each has its merits, the merit of each being in ways different from the other. As for the *ma'rifa* that is a consequence of love, it is indeed *ma'rifa* but they term it contemplation (*mushāhada*). Yet contemplation is other than *ma'rifa* in that *ma'rifa* on its own indicates a certain remoteness, contrary to contemplation [which indicates nearness]. There are divergences [of opinion] between the people of those states as to which is superior to the other, unveiling [*mukāshafa*] or contemplation [*mushāhada*]? The difference between these two terms is similar to that between the previous two in as much as one of them is taken to refer to general and the other to particular things, or one to principles and the other to branches. Unveiling is more general and contemplation more particular.[56] Our opinion regarding those two is similar to that regarding the first two.[57] And God knows best.

127

> The scholar 'Abdallāh ibn Muḥammad ibn 'Uthmān al-'Amūdī asked him whether one's obedience to one's parents' instructions still applies when they instruct one to pursue worldly means and widen one's use of permissible things, which may lead to some harm.

He answered: You ask about a person's duty to obey his parents and it is indeed so. If either of them instructs him to widen his use of permissible worldly things and occupy himself with the worldly means which may result in harm to his religion or expose him to falling into sinning against his Lord, then we believe and declare that he is not to obey them in that, but neither is he to antagonize them, nor confront them with a direct refusal or contradiction. On the contrary, he should avoid that and treat them with the gentleness and benevolence which he is obliged to show them. He is not to obey them in disobeying God since there should be "no obedience to a creature in disobeying The Creator,"[58] and since the above mentioned things are the precursors and means leading to sin and means falling under the same rules as their ends. "Those who roam around the ravine may easily fall into it."[59] Furthermore, the permissible things and worldly means of our times, which may be said, by those whose knowledge of the Book and *Sunna* is superficial, to be permissible, have become either forbidden or suspect, under the influence of the misunderstanding and confusion through which the people of this time perceive their religion. Those who possess insight into religion, are deeply steeped in the sciences of the Book and *Sunna*, and have certainty and *taqwā*, have no doubts about such things. Know this and reflect on it. You will, by God's Will, be happy and rightly guided. The whole thing is God's, there is neither power nor ability save by Him, He is our sufficiency and the Best of Custodians.

128

The Sufi Shaykh 'Abdallāh ibn Sa'īd al-'Amūdī asked him about what would happen should a *walī* do something which damages his integrity.

He answered: You ask whether if a *walī* commits something that damages his integrity such as a major sin, does not persist, that is, repents, fulfilling the inward and outward conditions of a sound repentance, he would maintain his station and state of sainthood. Know that if you mean the general *wilāya* which belongs to the generality of believers, then that may be so; there are many proofs to support this and these are so evident and well known that they need not be mentioned here. But if you mean by *wilāya* that of the elite, the possessor of which is said to be protected against disobedience, then know that such a *wilāya* is an immense thing and that its possessor never indulges in permissible and pleasurable things, let alone falls into minor sins. They [i.e., scholars] state that it is possible for such a *walī* to do such things only to prevent the implication that *awliyā'* share the Prophets' infallibility which allows them no sins whatsoever in any situation. So know that that which is possible is different from that which actually occurs, not everything that is possible does in effect occur. But, were we to assume that a *walī* of the elite does commit such acts, then it would diminish him greatly and he may be dispossessed of his state and station. This is indicated by the fact that some possessors of such stations committed permissible acts which put a barrier between them and their stations and diminished their degrees; this is well known by those who have studied their histories. We have already clarified this matter in answer to a question not dissimilar to yours; this is to be found near the beginning of the collection of legal opinions about matters we were asked about, compiled by the venerable *sayyid* Aḥmad ibn Zayn al-Ḥabashī. If these are in your possession then look into them, if not, then what we have given you in this concise answer is sufficient.

Sins and acts of disobedience, whether minor or major, are but filth, impurities and dirt from which God has purified His *awliyā'*, kept away from them, and raised their ranks above these occurring to them or their souls longing for them, let alone their actually committing them. Those sins which some said they fell into are sins in their acts of obedience and their stations, they only call them so because of their high degrees and sublime ranks, since the good deeds of the righteous are the misdeeds of the near; and you may have come across some of these utterances where they confess their shortcomings, their humility before their Lord, and the unworthiness of their ranks in relation to their witnessing. Know this for it is important and many make mistakes who have not studied these sciences thoroughly nor established themselves firmly in the stations of the people of authority. Where are the stars compared with the dust!? Where are the rubbish heaps compared to the company of kings!?

> Take what you know and leave what you hear.
> When the sun rises you no longer need Saturn.

May God grant us and you the best of His Solicitude and look at us always with the eye of His concern.

129

He was also asked by one of his close companions about things that will be clear in the answer.

He answered: Your blessed letter has arrived, artfully comprising sciences and subtleties that are witness to the uprightness of your tongue and heart and have joined subtlety of meanings to beauty of expression. Included in what you say in your letter is your inquiry about whether a man who is authorized to invest with the *khirqa* by a perfect shaykh, but sees himself unworthy of it, may perform the investiture; and this is followed by other important questions for which you are seeking answers. As things are, we shall now answer the important ones with clear concise answers, then, God willing, provide you with full expositions next year, for your letter only reached us just before our departure, at a time subject to dispersion and to events in forms that affect their world, which they manifest.[60] Once this is said, let us begin in briefly answering the important among those questions, we shall therefore say: it is permissible for one authorized by a recognized shaykh to invest with the *khirqa* even if he feels himself unworthy of it. His feeling of unworthiness adds to his perfection and compensates for whatever deficiencies might actually be there. He should maintain the conditions of investiture imposed by his shaykh, if any, both in the act itself and the person asking to be invested. He may also authorize others to carry on the investiture; this becomes an obligation if ever he comes to fear that the Path, as transmitted through that particular chain, threatens to disappear. Out of courtesy with his shaykh, he may act on his behalf, being the mediator between the shaykh and those he invests.

As for the words of our master, the *Quṭb*, the gnostic Abū-Bakr ibn 'Abdallāh al-'Aydarūs 'Alawī: "...to him is our *taḥkīm*,"[61] it appears that it means that his father is the total well-grounded shaykh from whom we derive our *taḥkīm*[62] and to whom we owe it, whom we emulate and whose method we follow, contrary to what Shaykh Baḥraq thought.

As for the investiture of our master al-Muqaddam by Shaykh Abū-Madyan, it was not done by the Shaykh's own hand but Shaykh 'Abdallāh al-Ṣāliḥ and 'Abdal-Raḥmān al-Maghribī were the mediators between them. This is what the shaykhs have mentioned.

130

As for your saying: "Is it permissible for a man who fears ostentation to teach [religious] sciences?" I say: Yes, it is permissible and it may even become incumbent if there is no one else to do it. He must, while doing so, strive against his own ego to abandon ostentation and become sincere and he must repent and seek forgiveness for any such thoughts or feelings that may occur to him. The accursed Devil—may God curse him!—wishes by this confusion to deprive Muslims of knowledge and action and of enjoining [good] and forbidding [evil]. Usually, those who fear ostentation are not ostentatious, but those who are and persistently remain so receive no reward. They may in addition become sinful, they are neither rewarded for teaching, nor for guiding others and inviting them to goodness, for these are part of teaching. But I hope that God will allow such a one to benefit from the prayers of those he teaches if they do pray and ask forgiveness for him. The rules governing the matter of ostentation were fully expounded by our Imām and the Imām of all Muslims, our master al-Ghazālī in the eighth chapter of the volume on "Ruinous Things" in the "*Iḥyā*'". Look into it and join to this the chapter on sincerity which is the seventh in the volume on "Saving Things." Cures for every ailment are there to be found.

131

As for your question concerning the bodies of the people of the Garden and their speech, and whether or not they are as the bodies and speech that we know in this world, I say: Yes, they are the same way that we know our bodies, speech, eating, drinking and so on. It is not permissible to think otherwise [since one should conform in his beliefs to] the outward meaning of the Book and *Sunna* and avoid interpretations. However, the bodies of the people of the Garden are greater than the present bodies, as mentioned [in the *Sunna*] and their perceptions much vaster, to the extent that, as has reached us, the vision of a person in the Garden perceives at a distance of seventy years in all directions. They also possess in sexual intercourse, eating, and other matters, an immense range appropriate to their situation. As for those who believe that the bodies of the people of the Garden and their speech and pleasures are to be taken as formless meanings and spiritual perceptions, these are the beliefs of philosophers. The Proof of Islam said: "Everything that was said concerning things of the Hereafter is to be taken at face value, with no interpretation. The Attributes of God which may suggest comparability and are opposed to transcendence are taken according to one of two schools: either to refrain from interpretations and believe in transcendence, which is the predecessors' school, or wade into interpretation within the limits of what is appropriate to the

Majesty and transcendence of God." Our school is that of the predecessors.

132

As for your question about children: The children of Muslims are in the Garden, as for the children of idolaters, we think it is better to refrain [from advancing an opinion] and neither state that they will enter the Garden nor the Fire. There are many differing opinions on that matter, and you are perhaps aware of them. The state of the children of Muslims in the Garden is perfect and complete childhood, since no flaws exist in the Garden; they are as knowledgeable adults. This is what appears to us and we have, so far, come across nothing concerning this. Rewards for the deeds of Muslim children are recorded in their parents' leaves and their degree [in the Garden] is the same. If their parents are unworthy, either because they are disbelievers or for any other reason, then this will apply to those above them, whether immediate grandfather or more remote ancestor, or to those who raised and educated the child, such as guardian or just ruler. The reasons for which fathers are given these rewards are two, the first is that they have begotten [the children] and the second that they raised and educated them. If [a dead] child is offered a recitation [of Qur'ān] or anything similar, it will either increase his face in beauty, light and so on, or it will go to those to whom the rewards for the child's deeds are attributed. If something is dedicated to a living person, it will be added to his good deeds on the leaves [where these are recorded]. If the person to whom it is offered is unworthy, whether he be alive or dead, because of idolatry or any other similar thing, it will return to the offerer as if he had not offered it. These things are the result of studied opinions based on principles and rules, but you will seldom find an explicit text in the Book or *Sunna* referring to such matters; the most that you can find is a quotation from a scholar based on a studied opinion such as we have described.

133

As for your saying about the verse in the *Tā'iyya* poem of Shaykh ibn al-Fāriḍ and other utterances of similar meaning from some who belong to Sufism, that it may be understood that the intention of the speaker is to attribute to himself or others superiority over the Prophets (peace be on them): You are well aware that the consensus of the community is that Prophets are superior to absolutely everyone else. Those people [the Sufis] are of all people the most attached to the truth and to following the Book and *Sunna*. Those who say about them that they are prone to excessiveness and exaggeration in this direction are more truthful than those who attribute neglect and dissipation to them, but both are mistaken, so do give this statement the consideration it deserves. Indeed, some of them, overcome by spiritual states, have let words overflow from their tongues that may induce others to think what you have mentioned and other things as well, all of which are open to many different interpretations. The best way is to attribute these [utterances] to [the states of] overpowering, absorption, loss of discrimination, and having lost possession of the power to decide which is the condition for accountability.[63] A sufficient proof to support this from sound *ḥadith* is his saying (peace be upon him): "So happy was he to have found his riding camel after having lost hope of doing so, that, overcome with joy, he said: 'O God, You are my slave and I Your lord!'" This would have been unequivocal disbelief had he said it while believing it and in the possession of his powers of discrimination, but it became of no consequence when he was overcome with joy and lost his power of discrimination. Other proofs to this effect are very numerous and that is the best way to think of the people of God in these matters. The subject is vast and if God is to ordain a more elaborate answer we shall speak at length on this subject, for it is something that we long for and need. But if God does not ordain so, then what He has granted us and caused to be written in this letter will be a reminder and an explanation to the intelligent and perceptive, but the unintelligent fool or the envious denier will only increase in their hardness and aversion were the matter to be clarified further. The first unable to understand because of his foolishness, and the second unwilling to confess and be guided because of his envy and denial. Success is in God's Hand.

134

The superior Shaykh, the Sufi scholar 'Abdallāh ibn Muhammad Bā-'Uthmān al-'Amūdī asked him about the statement in the book "*Laṭā'if al-Minan*" that people who are wronged can be divided into those who avenge themselves and those who do not. Then he mentions the fourth category which is the highest degree and adds that in this category falls what happened to Ibrāhīm ibn Adham, adding that Shaykh Abul-'Abbās had then commented that that was not the essence of perfection, which was what the Companion Sa'īd ibn Zayd, one of the Ten[64], did. It appears to me that both the act of Ibrāhīm ibn Adham and that of the Companion were the essence of perfection, for the crime in each case was different. The woman had accused an eminent Companion of injustice, in public and in the presence of the governor, perfection there was what he did (may God be pleased with him) to prove that he was innocent and she was lying, whereas the culprit in Ibrāhīm's case attacked a part of his body while ignorant of who he was. This is the gist of the question.

He answered: You find unclear and ask about a certain story mentioned in the book *"Laṭā'if al-Minan"* of Shaykh ibn 'Atā'illāh al-Shādhilī (may God's mercy be on him). The story is that of Ibrāhīm ibn Adham (may God's mercy be on him) with the man who beat him on the head and he forgave him, and what Shaykh Abul 'Abbās al-Mursī (may God's mercy be on him) said about it. He said that the act of Sa'īd ibn Zayd, one of the Ten Companions of the Messenger of God (may God's blessings and peace be upon him) who were promised the Garden, when he invoked [God] against the woman who alleged that he had appropriated some of her land – the story is very well known – was more perfect than that of Ibrāhīm when he forgave. Indeed, the matter is as you said and the justification of it as you understood it. The summation of it is that the kind of behavior shown by Ibrāhīm is better and more appropriate in general and unconditionally, and conforms to what is stated in *sharī'a*: unconditional encouragement to forgive, except when such a contingency arises as happened with Sa'īd ibn Zayd. These are rare and particular instances. A similar or almost similar thing occurred with Sa'd ibn Abī Waqqāṣ (may God be pleased with him), another one of the Ten, with a man from Kūfa who had said about him things which detracted from his religion and integrity, he invoked [God] against him and was answered, for he was a man whose prayers were answered. Many such events are known about the Companions and the Followers, but these are only a few when compared with what is related of the forgiveness and pardon of the Prophets, *imāms*, and virtuous servants of God. The determining factor is as you have understood. When the injury is to a man in himself or worldly matters then forgiveness is the correct and better course, whereas if it concerns religion, and the inviolable boundaries of God, the correct course is retribution. All of that was related about the Messenger of God (may God's blessings and peace be upon him), [and is to be found] in his sayings and actions, as anyone who has thoroughly studied the Prophet's *Sunna* will know.

135

He also asked him something about extinction (*fanā'*) that the author had attributed in the same book to his Shaykh, Abul-'Abbās.

He answered: You also find unclear in the same book the author's quoting his Shaykh as saying that there must remain with the *walī* in his extinction a subtle remnant of individual consciousness that justifies his being responsible before God. That is indeed so, however it does not apply unconditionally to every [kind or degree] of extinction, but to the early stages of extinction before it becomes firmly established, and also its late stages if one is nearing the state of subsistence (*baqā'*). As for the extinction where there is overpowering and absorption, no [individual] consciousness remains with it, but this [kind of] extinction very rarely lasts. It is not the most superior state of extinction and a man should not expose himself to it, but it may occur without being either sought or intended, and those to whom it occurs are excusable. Al-Qushayrī mentions in his treatise that a shaykh once entered his house, in a time of famine, and observing food there said: "This is in my house, and people are in this state of poverty!" then he fainted; he lost his reason and consciousness, the power of discrimination returning to him only at the times when the obligatory ritual prayers were due; following which the same state overtook him again. Qushayrī, commenting on the state of that Shaykh, said that this was Divine protection and acceptable absorption in God. This is the meaning and gist of the story. The summation of the matter is that extinction includes states which are superior but not overpowering, and others which overpower the servant and take him until he becomes extinct to himself first, then extinct to his own extinction. These states are not unconditionally superior and much more can be said about the matter. Qushayrī in his Treatise and Suhrawardī in "'*Awārif*' have written about the state of extinction in a more elaborate way, so do read them, and what we have mentioned is sufficient for those who possess, as you do, intelligence and perspicacity to the full. And God knows best.

You also say that you long to visit and sit with us but are prevented from doing so by the attachment of your parents and the sadness they feel when you are away from them, especially your mother. This is indeed an excuse. Uways al-Qarnī (may God's mercy be on him) was delayed in meeting with the Messenger of God (may God's blessings and peace be upon him) and keeping his company, by his service to his mother, in loyalty and compassion for her. That added to his superiority but in a manner distinct from that which made the Companions superior to others. There are many kinds of superiority in many contexts. He said in *ḥadith* (may blessings and peace be upon him) to a man who sought his permission to go to battle *(jihād)*: "Your *jihād* is in them."[65] To the other who said to him: "I came to you and left them weeping."[66] He said: "Return to them and make them laugh as you made them weep." And to the one who mentioned his mother to him he said: "Stay at her feet, for there is the Garden." There are in religion things which are more important than others. Some may be possible for those who are keen but physically remote, others not so. A man who acquires the knowledge, and understands it, and has *taqwā* and behaves well, will not be unaware of how to discriminate between important and meritorious [but less important matters], priorities and preferences.

May God the Exalted expand our breasts and yours to *Islām* and *Īmān*, and make us of those who realize *taqwā* and *Iḥsān*, that we may win His company and love. "*God is with those who have taqwā and those who behave with excellence.*" [16:128] "*There is no fault in those who believe and do deeds of righteousness…*" up to "*…God loves those who act with excellence.*" [5:93][67]

136

A *sayyid* of his companions asked him about the saying of Shaykh Muḥyiddīn 'Abdal-Qādir al-Jīlanī (may God be pleased with him): "Every degree between the *Nāsūt* and the *Malakūt* is *sharī'a*, every degree between the *Malakūt* and the *Jabarūt* is *ḥaqīqa*, and every degree between the *Jabarūt* and the *Lāhūt* is *ma'rifa*."

He answered: Know that [the term] *Nāsūt* indicates the perceptible human world, *Malakūt* indicates the world that is unseen by both human and other beings, the interface between them is termed the world of *Mulk. Sharī'a* belongs to this world for it consists in upholding the truth and affirming actions and secondary causes in the manner they were affirmed by God. The interface between *Malakūt* and *Jabarūt* is *ḥaqīqa. Malakūt*, as stated before, is the unseen world and *Jabarūt* is part of it, that is *Jabarūt* is specific and *Malakūt* general. *Ḥaqīqa* is to see everything by God and for God, by way of direct experience (*dhawq*) and unveiling (*kashf*). The term *Jabarūt* is, as we have said, more specific than *Malakūt. Lāhūt* indicates the Names, Attributes, and Divine Essence. *Ma'rifa* is to contemplate these and see their reality unveiled. Thus whoever establishes *sharī'a* outwardly, and realizes *ḥaqīqa* inwardly, then contemplates the lights of the Names, Attributes, and Supreme Essence, he is the Perfect Man. *Sharī'a* is *Islām*, which is submission to God, *ḥaqīqa* is *Īmān* and certainty, it is sincerity with God, and *Ma'rifa* is *Iḥsān*, extinction by God in God. This is in brief what has appeared at this moment of the meaning of these words, all knowledge is with God and God knows best.

137

> A man from Madina asked him about the interpretation given by the gnostic Shaykh ibn 'Arabī in the "*Futūḥāt*" for the Prophet's saying (may blessings and peace be upon him) in the *ḥadith* of the *Dajjāl*, "A day as a week and a day as a month..."[68]

He answered: You said you were interested and keen to read the books of the gnostic Sufi Shaykh Muḥyiddīn Muḥammad ibn 'Alī bin 'Arabī and that you found problematic his interpretation of the meaning of the quoted *ḥadith* about the length of the period of the *Dajjāl*, and that you feared, because you found it problematic, that it may have been interpolated in the Shaykh's writings. Know that there are many problematic matters in the Shaykh's books, particularly in the "*Fuṣūṣ*" and the "*Futūḥāt*". These may have been either added to the Shaykh's writings, or produced by him when overpowered by a [spiritual] state and under the overwhelming power of a higher reality. It would then be the kind of immoderation (*shaṭḥ*) which, in those who are overwhelmed, is excusable. Or the Shaykh may have expressed it in such a manner as to conceal behind it secrets and meanings too subtle to be put into words, and in that case the form of the expressions would be obscure but their spirits and realities sound, firm and not at all farfetched. The words of the Shaykh which you found farfetched fall into one of those categories, by God's will. The Shaykh is one of those who have a firmly established stand in sciences, gnoses, fear of God, and renunciation of the world. It is inappropriate for anyone who fears God and knows about the Shaykh's state, that which we have just mentioned, to accuse him of straying from the truth, as some have done who had the audacity to do what they should not have. If you are to read some of the writings of this Shaykh and meet with pronouncements that you find problematic, just accept it and do not inquire further and seek farfetched interpretations or you will gain nothing but weariness. This is the counsel we give you and all those who look into this Shaykh's books and those of others like him, who are people of *ḥaqīqa* and have expressed it in their books. Those who do not comply and accept what we say are not safe from falling into the greater or smaller errors. May God the Exalted make us and you firm with the firm words, and of those who recognize the truth, hold on and conform to it, and recognize falsehood, avoid and cast it away. Reflect on these words, for within them are important warnings which need elaborations too lengthy for a letter of this size. The best of speech is that which is brief yet informative.

138

> *Sayyid* Abū-Bakr ibn 'Alī Ibrāhīm al-Baytī asked him about the saying of Shaykh Yaḥyā ibn Mu'ādh al-Rāzī: "Abandon all the world and you will find all the world. To take it is to abandon it and to abandon it is to take it."

He answered: The words are clear and show not the least obscurity. They mean that whoever abandons the whole world in renunciation, God will compensate him with repose both in his heart due to giving up avidity and preoccupation, and in his body due to giving up striving and seeking. Reasonable men wish only for repose in the world, for this do people strive and aspire outwardly and inwardly, but they miss the way to it which is only found by the renunciates. This is indicated by his saying (may God's blessings and peace be upon him): "Renouncing the world rests the heart and body, while the wish for it increases worry and sadness." A sage was once asked: "To whom does the world belong?" He said: "To those who abandon it." And:

"To whom does the Hereafter belong?" He said: "To those who pursue it."

139

> The same *sayyid* asked him about the words of our master Abū-Bakr al Ṣiddīq in counseling 'Umar as he made him his successor: "And know, O 'Umar, that God has works to be done by day which He does not accept by night, and works by night which He accepts not by day."

He answered: This is also clear, for most works have specific times and are acceptable only then. If requited at a later time they fall under a different ruling and need other conditions for their acceptance. Furthermore some of the things to be done by day involve created beings and the needs of the people are mostly to be seen to by day, therefore if a man does not attend to them in time, without an excuse, they are not accepted from him. As for his saying: "No supererogatory act is accepted until the obligatory ones are fulfilled," it is clear, for obligatory acts are binding rights [to be fulfilled] whereas supererogatory ones are freely willed additions; the fulfillment of rights have priority over freely willed additions, both as concerns the dues of the Real and those of creation. This is a summary that bears much detailing.

140

> And he asked him about how to reconcile his two sayings (may peace be upon him): "People will be gathered at the resurrection barefoot, naked, uncircumcised." And: "The Community (*Umma*) will be gathered in their shrouds."

He answered: First of all, one has to accept the sounder of the two *ḥadiths*. If they are of the same degree of soundness then the gathering in their shrouds would be taken to be particular to this Community or to a particular group of it. The term Community, may be used in many ways and the term people is of wider meaning. I believe the *ḥadith*: "People will be gathered barefoot..." is sounder than the other; it is also of wider meaning.[69]

141

> And he asked him whether when concluding a full recitation of the Qur'ān, *sūrat al-Ikhlās* should be read three, four, or one time.

He answered: It should be read once, as any other *sūra*, or four times, once as part of the full recitation and three in the hope of it being equal to a second full recitation. Should there be any shortcomings in the first recitation, it is our good hope that God will requite them with the second. The reciter should be the one to read it, no one else, which is better and more correct; the others are to listen to his recitation and recite with him. It has been soundly transmitted that the Prophet (may God's blessings and peace be upon him) said that to recite *Qul huwa'llāhu Aḥad* once equals one third of the Qur'ān. This means that to recite it thrice equals a full recitation and this is what we think. It is then to be recited once or four times, there is no justification for reciting it three times. And God knows best.

142

> The scholar 'Umar ibn 'Abdallāh ibn al-'Afīf al-Hajraynī asked him about the commentary of the Sufi Shaykh Ḥasan ibn Aḥmad Bā-Shu'ayb on a poem by the gnostic Shaykh 'Abdal-Hādī al-Sūdī, where at the mention of divestment he says: "An excellent mount divestment is, if he begins to come out of the six, leave the ten, cross the four, and concentrate on the One."

He answered: As for the One, that is God the Exalted. The six, ten, and four are numbers mentioned by the Shaykh to indicate things which the traveler should divest himself of. They are, generally speaking, either obstacles which are ahead of him, or attachments which are behind him, they cannot be specified unless heard from the commentator, for such things are numerous and one does not know what he meant by them. A sincere traveler should divest himself of them all and concentrate on the Real One with all his outward and inward.

His comment on that part of the poem where he says: 'Abandon attachments,' by saying: "Our Shaykh (meaning the *Quṭb* Shaykh Abū-Bakr ibn-Sālim Alawī) has said: 'Between you and God are ten veils, people constitute nine, while the ego, the devil, and all other obstacles constitute one veil.'" That is a matter where travelers differ. The Shaykh may have meant the one he was addressing or all those present on that particular occasion. There are great differences between people in that respect, some may even have only one veil, their ego, others may have seventy veils, or more, or less. It cannot be correctly said that they all have ten veils of which nine are the other people. Understand this! This is what has appeared to me, and God knows best.

143

> Shaykh 'Abdallāh ibn Sa'īd al-'Amūdī asked him whether the gnostic should reprove any of the created beings' acts.

He answered: Yes, he should reprove whatever the pure Law reproves, this is his duty along with other believers and Muslims, according to that which was expounded in the Law and stated by scholars in matters of enjoining good and forbidding evil. As for seeing the Acts of God compared with which the acts of created beings are nothing, the gnostic can deny nothing of them, neither by state nor because of the exaltation of his rank and perfection of his state. This applies to him in particular and to all other Muslims in general. He who neither enjoins good as defined in the Law nor forbids evil as defined in the Law, has disobeyed and misbehaved, he has no firm position in either *sharīʿa* or *ḥaqīqa*.

The one in a state of extinction, whose outward and inward are both absorbed in the state that has descended on him (*wārid*), is in the same legal position as those for whom the pen holds off from recording [their deeds] such as the sleeper, etc., until he comes to and regains his powers of discrimination and reasoning. Beware of becoming inclined to the utterances of those who err and speak immoderately, there are on their part repugnant matters which come near to heresy and transgressing [the limits of] religion.[70]

144

The superior scholar ʿAbdallāh ibn Muḥammad ibn ʿUthmān al-ʿAmūdī asked him about a statement which he found obscure: "The gnosis (*maʿrifa*) of a perfect man is incomplete until he knows what is his, what is from him, in him, and incumbent on him, and he fulfills all these; and that he knows what was before creation and what was not, and what was to be before his creation and after it, that which never was and how it would have been had it been, and when would all that be." He then made that knowledge a condition for the perfection of gnosis. The scholar then added: "What I feel is that the gnosis that gives its possessor the title of gnostic is the knowledge of what is necessarily God's, what is for Him impossible and what is possible, not by way of proofs and logical arguments but through unveiling (*kashf*) and contemplation (*mushāhada*). His saying: '...until he knows what is his,' etc., concerns the knowledge of something of the Unseen and is not a condition for gnosis. His saying: 'and knows what was...' I found very problematic, for that can only be true for God, Transcendent and Exalted is He! Should we suppose that some of that knowledge is given to one whom God favors with some of His secrets, it is still a condition neither for gnosis itself nor for its perfection."

He answered: The passage that you have come across stating that gnosis is not complete for a perfect man, etc., and which you found problematic, is indeed problematic. If the speaker is not a recognized imām in this field then we do not accept his statement because it contains obscurities and mistakes which are neither factual nor possible. If he is one of the comprehensive imāms then it would be attributed to immoderation (*shaṭḥ*) and being overwhelmed, or to using these expressions loosely in such a way as to substitute partial matters and details for inclusive and general ones. This may happen in their expressions in particular and the expressions of the Arabs in general, as is known to those who have thorough and wide knowledge of the general and particular aspects of that matter. Your definition of the state of the gnostic is good and convincing. Reflect on what we have said; it is concise and carries within it details that will appear with thoughtful scrutiny. And God knows best.

145

One of the people attached to him asked him about a man who used to see one of the *awliyā* in his dreams then stopped doing so, would this be due to some defect in him or to something else. What effective remedies should he use to correct this defect?

He answered: You ask about a man who used to see in his dreams a certain man of virtue (may God have mercy on them and let us and you benefit from them!) and now no longer does: know that dream-visions (*ru' yā*) are good tidings, as stated in *ḥadith*, they are also warnings and admonitions for those who heed them and who profit from warnings. If he was used to seeing the man and then was deprived of it, it indicates that his degree has diminished. He should repent and abundantly ask for forgiveness and pray on the Messenger of God (may God's blessings and peace be upon him and on his noble family). A gnostic once said: "One of the most profitable invocations for the people of this time in particular is to abundantly ask for forgiveness and invoke blessings and peace on the Chosen Prophet." May the blessings of God the Benevolent and Merciful and His peace be on him, his House, Companions, and those who follow them with excellence till the Day of Judgment, when people arise before the Lord of the Worlds. This is the answer that has appeared to this *faqīr* at this time where hearts are suffering from confusing interferences, and sins and defects have become excessive. We ask The One Who knows all that is hidden to forgive us and you.

146

A disciple of knowledge asked him about the saying of the gnostic Shaykh Aḥmad ibn 'Abdallāh ibn Abil-Khiyār (may God have mercy on him): "The alighting station of the letter *Zāy*, and the presence of the *Dāl*, the letter of perfection, honor, and pride."

He answered: In the name of God the Giver of Openings, the Knower. Praise belongs to God the Munificent, the Generous. May God grant His blessings and peace to our master and patron Muhammad, the guide to the straight path.

This matter belongs to the science of signs. To express it explicitly renders it even more obscure, even if done by the author himself. If the author is a man of reality and realization who has combined knowledge with traveling the Path, then let one take the blessing of hearing his words and believe that they are the reality and the truth. In this way one may benefit even if one does not understand that which they indicate and at which they aim. There is safety in acceptance and everything good is in realizing *taqwā* and maintaining rectitude. And God knows best.

147

He also asked him whether in seeking beneficial sciences one would best read many books, meet with scholars or use his intelligence and understanding?

He answered: One would be acting in sincerity and excellence in doing all these, having first formed the virtuous intention of seeking knowledge, being sincere with God while doing so, and aiming to benefit him and others. The one who combines all these will be a distinguished disciple of knowledge for whom openings are to be hoped for as well as the achievement of his aim in the most appropriate way. The one who does not combine them all but is of good intention and sincere with God, will attain to his share of the quest. "*Each has a degree according to what they have done, and your Lord is not unaware of the things they do*." [6:132]

148

He also asked him about the sign of an answered prayer and about other things, which will appear in the answer.

He answered: Let it be known, first of all, that every prayer from a pious believer who turns to God is answered, but the answer is either immediate or delayed, and God, in His solicitude for His servant, may give him what is better, but different from what he has prayed for. There are verses of the Qur'ān and *ḥadiths*, sound and weaker, to that effect. They have also mentioned as signs of the prayer being answered a shiver and a cooling off of the heart as concerns his eagerness to ask for what he has prayed for. There are obstacles and circumstances which may prevent a prayer being answered, among which are to eat or wear something *ḥarām*, to persist in treating others unjustly, to pray while distracted from God, for he has said (may God's blessings and peace be upon him): "Know that God does not answer the prayer of a distracted heart," to have severed one's kinship bonds, or quarreled with a fellow believer and broken relations with him unjustly.

As for the question about one who has asked his Lord for things and seen some of them fulfilled, would this be a sign that all others would be answered as well, yes, it is a sign of that if you take into account hope, the vastness of Divine Generosity, and thinking-well of God. It may also not be a sign of that for reasons which have to do with either the man who prays or the thing he prays for. This is the answer that has appeared for the time being, and God knows best. These things need elaboration, they are comprehensive and it would be too lengthy to detail them. The best of words are those which are brief yet informative. God is The Helper.

149

He also asked him about the 'resting pause' (*jalsat'al-istirāḥa*)[71].

He answered: Many scholars have spoken about it (may God's mercy be on them) and what we feel inclined to accept is what was said by Shaykh Aḥmad ibn 'Umar al-Ḥubayshī as well as by *sayyid* Muḥammad al-Barzanjī, for it avoids constraint and the kind of [overzealous] inquiry that is discouraged in most matters. Let him who has asked know that the 'resting pause' is a matter about which early scholars have differed as to whether or not it is a *Sunna*. Those who say it is not a *Sunna* say that it was done by the Messenger of God (may God's blessings and peace be upon him) in his last days when he had become heavy and found some difficulty in rising after prostration. Furthermore, those who affirm it say that it is extremely brief, just enough to say *Subḥān Allāh*; some even say that one should merely prolong the *takbīr* starting from when one begins to rise from prostration and ending with the completion of the movement. This they did not consider an excessive prolongation since the 'resting pause' is to be so brief. If this is the way things are, then one should not think too much with such obsessiveness about whether his prayer is valid or not, the way he should take differences of opinion into consideration, and other such things. He has said (peace be upon him) "The excessive will perish!" He repeated it thrice. Let the man engaged in ritual prayer be concerned to the utmost and concentrate on his presence of heart and humility before God in his prayer, and on emptying his breast from all obsessions and thoughts of the world which threaten to absorb him when he prays and prevent him from being present and humble; and God knows best.

150

As for your question concerning dedicating one's reward for a monetary charity to the dead, whether one's parents or otherwise, it is something that should be done and was transmitted in *ḥadith*. One has to invoke blessings on the Messenger then say: "O God, give the reward for this – specifying what it is – to the spirit of so and so or [the spirits] of so and so and so and so!" As for recitations [of Qur'ān] there are differences between scholars as to whether the rewards for them reach the dead. It seems that the position of Imām al-Shāfi'ī (may God have mercy on him) and others, is that it does not, but some of his disciples were of the opinion that it does. So let the person say: "O God give the reward for what I have recited of this *ḥizb* or *sūra* [to be specified] to the spirit of so and so." This should be done with only a portion of his charity and a portion of whatever Qur'ān he recites, but he should keep most of it to himself. This is how we see the matter and what is deduced from the opinions of scholars. Whatever is recited for a fee has to be dedicated wholly to those who pay the fee. As for your hearing someone say: "And inscribe a reward similar to it in our record," this is a prayer which may or may not be answered. The angel who says "Amen! And to you the same!" concerns the prayer of a believer for his brother in his absence, it should not be generalized. Common people are sometimes correct, but more often than not they are mistaken in their words and deeds. This is our stance in this matter; and God and His Messenger know best.

151

> He was asked about such expressions used by the Sufis as 'the light of the intellect', 'the light of knowledge' and 'the light of the truth', whether these lights were different spirits that enter the heart or nothing but the intellect which acts as a mirror where appear the lights of knowledge of different kinds, gnostic knowledge and inspirations, being then the source of them all, like the seeing eye where bodies are reflected and the beholder gains from that the knowledge of them. Do clarify for this yearning person this well guarded secret.

He answered: Praise is for God. We have seen your blessed question which indicates the need and thirst of the questioner for knowing the truth which hits the mark, the answer and his own acceptance of it. Let the questioner know, may God grant him success, that the multiplicity of lights is nothing to be surprised about when it often occurs in the expressions of the sufis and others, or when it occurs in reality. The gist of it is that between the mentioned lights there are certain differences which necessitate both their multiplicity and their being different degrees, each above the other. You may say: "The light of the eyesight, the light of the inner eyesight, and the light of the secret," and this will bring out the multiplicity and the differences. One may ask, concerning this example, whether the secret is the same as the inner eyesight. We say: one is general and the other specific, for the [term] secret is general while the [term] inner eyesight is specific. Much can be said about this; Imām al-Ghazālī has written a book entitled: "The Niche of Lights" where he mentions the lights and their degrees as well as many other subtle things from the sciences of truth and reality. And God knows best and is Wiser.

152

You have asked, may God reform your affairs, about the seventy and the eight mentioned by our master the gnostic Imām Abul-Ḥasan al-Shādhilī (may God be pleased with him) in *Ḥizb al-Nūr* (the Litany of Light) once in the context of supplication and then in that of asking for protection. The seventy and the eight for whose sake he is beseeching [God to grant him something] are necessarily different from the seventy and the eight from which he seeks protection. There is a wide scope for interpretation in both contexts, in the first the mentioned numbers may be Prophets, angels, some of the Most Excellent Names of God, and so on. The numbers mentioned in the second context may be attributes of the 'inciting soul', incidental ailments, demons, and so on. We say: The one who prays [using such formulae] should form the intention of conforming to the meaning that the Shaykh to whom the litany belongs intended. This is wider and more complete, for the Shaykh is a trustworthy gnostic possessing the *'ilm ladunnī*, the knowledge of the gnostics. And God knows best.

153

He was also asked how one should recite the litanies of our master Shaykh Abul-Ḥasan al-Shādhilī.

He answered: Know that a certain gnostic once said that *Ḥizb al-Baḥr* (the Litany of the Sea) should be regularly recited after each ritual prayer. Another, and I think it was ibn bint al-Maylaq, one of the comprehensive Shādhilī shaykhs, said that one should recite *Ḥizb al-Barr* after the dawn prayer, this being the greater *Ḥizb* of Shaykh Abul-Ḥasan, which he called the Greatest Alchemy, *Ḥizb al-Nūr* after the midday prayer, *Ḥizb al-Baḥr* after the afternoon prayer, *Ḥizb al-Tawḥīd* after the sunset prayer, all these being Shaykh Abul-Ḥasan's, and *Ḥizb al-Ḥamd wal Shukr* after the night prayer, this one belonging to Shaykh Abul-'Abbās al-Mursī, the Shaykh's disciple and heir. These should be recited in the best possible state, which is in ritual purity, orientation [toward the *Qibla*], humble submission and presence of the heart with God. In that manner will the aimed for benefit and enlightening of the heart occur. One should also precede them with [the invocations] that were transmitted from the Messenger (may God's blessings and peace be upon him) whether verses [of the Qur'ān], invocations, or prayers to follow each ritual prayer. This is what was stated by those who were concerned with this subject. The secret is to be sincere in concentration, firmly resolute, and of pure intention.

154

He was asked about things that will become clear from the answer.

He answered: You ask about the state of the three persons who came to a circle of *dhikr*, one of whom found an empty place and occupied it, the second of whom sat outside the circle, and the third of whom went away. To all appearances, the state of the first one is praiseworthy and good, that of the second is not far from that, since to show shyness before God is honorable and irreproachable; the third, who went away, deserves to be censured and this turning away may well lead him to sin if it is due to arrogance and belittling the *dhikr* and those who do it. But if it is out of distraction or neglect of good things then it is enough that he has missed his being remembered, praised and rewarded by God. Circles where the Great Qur'ān [is recited] and those where profitable religious knowledge [is taught] are indeed circles of remembrance in its wider meaning for every man who obeys God and is occupied with that which draws him nearer to Him, Exalted is He. This was stated by scholars such as Imām al-Nawawī in his book "*al-Adhkār*" and others.

His saying (may God's blessings and peace be upon him): "Morning comes on people and on each of their phalanges a charity is due." This is a charity that originates in thankfulness and how to be thankful to perfection. It seems that it is not an offence not to do this, but is to be attributed to distraction and described as a shortcoming in giving God the Exalted His due of thanks. This is why he said (may God's blessings and peace be upon him) in one version of the *ḥadith*: "...and whoever does that will have inched himself away from the Fire." And in another: "and this is fulfilled by two *rak'as* performed in mid-morning (*Duḥā*)." These are meritorious acts that a servant profits from and that draw him nearer to his Lord, for all the things mentioned in this *ḥadith* are supererogatory devotions that lead one nearer to God.

As for his saying (peace be on him): "Look for me among the weak." These are the destitute and the feeble among virtuous believers. The Messenger of God (may

God's blessings and peace be upon him) loved them, sat in their company, and said: "You are given rain and provision because of the weak among you." And for them were revealed His words, Exalted is He: "*And restrain thyself with those who call upon their Lord at morning and evening, desiring His Face…*" [18:28] And: "*And do not drive away those who call upon their Lord at morning and evening, desiring His Face.*" [6:52] And the beginning of *sūra 'Abasa* (He Frowned). These are all statements to that effect which explain the matter. This is what has appeared to us at the present moment and what is to be understood from the opinions of other scholars (may God have mercy on them). God and His Messenger know best.

155

He was questioned about the Prophet's saying (may God's blessings and peace be upon him): "*Subḥān Allāhi wa biḥamdihi 'adada khalqihi…*" (Transcendent is God and praised by His praise [to Himself] as much as the number of all His creatures…) and whether the same reward is obtained by repeating the same formula with *takbīr* and *tahlīl*.

He answered: That which he specifically mentioned (may God's blessings and peace be upon him) is not to be equated with anything else. However, should a sincere servant do this [i.e., use the formula in the said manner] hoping [in God's mercy], for the graces of God are immense, he will either receive the reward for it or at any rate some of it. "*God allows not the reward of those whose works are excellent to go to waste.*" [9:120]

156

To another question asked by someone who was attached to him, he answered: You inquire about the *ḥadith* stating that each verse [of the Qur'ān] has an outward, an inward, a limit and a rising place. Scholars have discussed this at length, for instance Imām al-Ghazālī in the "*Iḥyā*'" and "*al-Arbe'īn*", Abū Ṭālib al-Makkī, the author of "'*Awārif*" as well, I think, and others. Much can be said about this matter, however, it is unimportant to inquire about it because most of it relates to the sciences of the outward.

As for the question about the invocations and prayers to be said during the night's supererogatory prayers (*tahajjud*), we use this formula after the two light *rak'as* and this is the best time for it. It is different from the invocation and prayer that are said after waking up, passing the hands over one's face, and lifting one's face toward heaven, these I use when I wake up and before the ritual purification. We have noticed that the author of "*Tuhfat al-Muta'abbid*" has quoted the prayer that begins: *Allāhumma laka'l-ḥamdu, anta qayyūmu'l-samāwāti wa l-arḍ*, etc., among the prayers to be said at the beginning [of the ritual prayer]. There does not seem to be any reason for that, so let it be used after the two light *rak'as*.

As for the *sūras* which are, according to *ḥadith* to be recited every night such as *Ya-Sīn*, *al-Jinn*, *al-Dukhān*, *al-Mulk* and *al-Wāqi'a*, they are better recited during the first part of the night. If, for any reason, one is prevented from doing so then let it be on awakening. This is what we do at those times when we sleep early or are prevented by another reason. These were our answers to your questions according to what we saw at that time, and God and His Prophet know best.

157

'Umar ibn Sālim Bā-Ḥumayyid inquired about things which will become apparent from the answer and was answered:

As for your question about the *Maghrib* prayer being performed very soon [after the Call] in this blessed month,

Ramaḍān, so that one worries that were he to break his fast with anything more than water, such as dates for instance, he would need to wash his mouth thoroughly to remove their traces and may thus miss the initial *takbīr* [*takbīr al-iḥra̱m*] or even more [of the prayer than that]. To hasten to break one's fast and to do so before the *Maghrib* prayer is a *Sunna* which both earlier and later generations have upheld. This can be done with water if one fears missing [part of the prayer] as you have mentioned for the reason that you have mentioned. As for breaking the fast with dates or something similar, it is another *Sunna*. If that is done after the prayer for the mentioned reason then it does not make much difference. What we think is best is to break the fast with dates, then water, then prayer, giving each its due.

As for your having heard one of the common people say, having heard the caller (*mu'azzin*) say: "There is no divinity other than God (*lā ilāha illa'llāh*)", "Yes, there is no divinity save God!" your approval of it, and your inquiry about whether anything was transmitted concerning this, know that we have heard about no transmissions concerning this and it is better to follow the *Sunna*. Habits even if worthy of approval cannot be depended on if different from the transmitted *Sunnas*.

158

And you inquired about the speaker saying, when mentioning crops and plants during the prayer for rain: "And protect them from many afflictions!" It seems that you understood that He will protect them from many but not all afflictions, this is not so, for the sentence means: "Protect them from all afflictions, and these are many." Many here serving to indicate the multitude of afflictions not that they are divided. He put afflictions after many to maintain the rhyme [in his prose] because it has more effect on people, especially in sermons. Had he just said afflictions and neither added many nor few, as he has done elsewhere, it would have been good, but this is better from the point of view of eloquence and rhythm. He has also said in one of his *Ramadan* sermons: "I fulfilled in you many wishes." Meaning my wishes which were many. Think about it for it is clear.

159

As for your inquiry about the sins that people commit in the month of *Ramaḍān* despite the devils being shackled, know that it has been mentioned in a *ḥadith* that the ones who are shackled are the worst among them, and if that is so then no problem exists. But if [the shackling] concerns all of them then it is the soul, for the 'soul which incites to evil' commits sins all by itself, especially under some circumstances and in matters which it lusts after. Scholars have mentioned such thoughts which are independent [of the devil's insinuations] and similar things were alluded to by Shaykh Ibn 'Arabī.

As for your saying: "only the Perfect Man, that is the *Quṭb*, the *Ghawth*, can pray the perfect prayer," this is not so. We say: Those belonging to the Circle of Sainthood and the elect among believers perform their prayers perfectly, but they differ in the degree of their perfection in performing them, in other devotions and in concentrating on Divinity. In this matter the Perfect Man is the most accomplished and complete among them since he faces the special Saintly Presence which is the Presence of Unicity (*Ḥaḍrat al-Aḥādiyya*). When one becomes perfect, his prayers and acts of worship become perfect. Praise to God, all good is God's, He gives whom He wills, favors whom He wills, and He is the One of great favors. And God knows best.

160

The righteous scholar, the illumined Shaykh, possessor of both the knowledge and the practice of it,

'Abdallāh ibn 'Uthmān al-'Amūdī asked him questions to which he answered:

The answers to the questions which you pose in the letter that arrived with your illumined son Sa'īd are clear and should not be obscure for someone such as you. However, we shall briefly discourse on them so that problems, if any, will be solved. As for your inquiry about it having been transmitted that the Garden of Eden is the summit of the Garden and overlooking all the other Gardens, I cannot remember ever having heard of it. What is well known about Firdaws and Eden is that they are the navel and center of the Garden. There is, however, no contradiction between the two and, if the first transmission is sound, they can easily be combined. It has been transmitted that Firdaws is the highermost part of the Garden and that its roof is the Throne of the All-Merciful. There is a prayer of the Prophet where he says: "O God! I ask You for that Garden the shade of which is Your Throne, the light of which is Your Face, and the content of which is Your Mercy." It is enough for the believing servant simply to ask God for the Garden, especially when his knowledge, behavior, and sincerity are as those of the elect of this time. It has reached us that the Imām Ibn al-Mubārak (may God have mercy on him) came out to meet his friends one day saying: "I was so impudent with my Lord last night that I asked him for the Garden." There is also the *ḥadith* of the bedouin who said: "I know nothing of your droning and that of Mu'ādh; I just ask God for the Garden and His protection against the Fire." He replied (may God's blessings and peace be upon him): "Around these do we drone."

161

You ask about his saying (may God's blessings and peace be upon him): "Were I and the Son of Mary to be judged for what these two have committed…"[72] meaning the index finger and thumb, despite their being infallible noble Messengers. There is nothing obscure in this, for the rights of God on His servants can be fulfilled by none, not even a Near Angel or a Messenger and Prophet. The elect have sins appropriate to their ranks, such as looks and thoughts even at times of devotions; almost no human being is safe from these. Look at the stories of Adam, Abraham, David, and Solomon (may peace be upon them), which are mentioned in the Qur'ān and *ḥadith*, and you will understand the meaning of his words (may God's blessings and peace be upon him). We had referred briefly to such matters in answering a letter written to us by a *sayyid* from al-Shiḥr, you may perhaps have it in your collection of letters. In the *ḥadith* of intercession are also references to this, when people go to Adam and the matter ends up with the lord of all Messengers.

162

As for your inquiry about the *ḥadith* where it is mentioned that: "The one who stands up [in prayer] with ten verses will not be recorded among the distracted…" until: "…and the one who stands up [in prayer] with a thousand verses is recorded among the very rich." This *ḥadith* is very well known. The evident meaning is that it refers to praying at night, for most of our virtuous predecessors' nocturnal recitations of the Qur'ān were during ritual prayers, as was authentically transmitted about him (may God's blessings and peace be upon him) and the predecessors among the community [by which are meant] the Companions and Followers. As for recitations outside the ritual prayers, whether diurnal or nocturnal, it was said in a sound *ḥadith* that each letter counted as a good deed. And according to the Commander of the Faithful 'Alī ibn Abī Ṭālib (may God honor his face) the one who recites the Qur'ān standing up in prayer has each letter counted as one hundred good deeds, if sitting down in prayer then fifty good deeds, if outside prayer but in a state of ritual purity then twenty five good deeds, if not in a state of purity then for each letter ten good deeds. Such statements made by a Companion never originate in him; they are therefore given the value of a connected [*marfū'*] *ḥadith*. There are on this subject *ḥadiths* which may give the impression that they contradict each other and that the reciter receives rewards for a [diversity of recorded] good deeds; there is nothing unlikely or impossible about that, for the grace of God is vast, and people differ in their degrees as far as recitation as well as other things are concerned, so ascribe the differences [in reward] to the differences [in performance]. "*Each shall have their degrees according to what they have done. We shall pay them in full and they shall not be wronged.*" [46:19]

163

As for your question concerning those virtuous servants of God who are 'people of misbehavior' (*ahl al-takhrīb*)[73], the people subject to the 'Divine Attraction', whose minds have become overwhelmed by the realities which appeared to them and which they were unable to bear; they feared they might become known and that people may become attached to them so they hid behind some of that [kind of reprehensible behavior]. We say: These times are as Qushayrī, followed by Ibn 'Arabī, said in their writings. Qushayrī said:

> "As for the tents they resemble theirs
> But I see that the women of the place are unlike theirs."[74]

As for Ibn 'Arabī, he said: "Qushayrī said this because he saw those who imitated their manners without following their guidance. As for now, there are neither women nor tents." Today they have gone and so have their traces and manners. Nothing remains but their tales, the pardon of God, and thinking-well of all believers, in general and in particular.

All people are now 'people of misbehavior', rare are those who still firmly maintain their Unification, prayers, *zakāt*, fasts, and *ḥajj*, as you can see and hear. May God help us! If anyone is still found who is said to be in that state you inquired about, to whom virtue is attributed, whose Unification is firm and who is careful to establish the ritual prayer and similar rules of religion, who avoids major sins such as adultery, ostentation, dispossessing others of their wealth and associating with the iniquitous and those who persist in transgressions, then he falls into any kind of minor misdeeds such as looking at women, listening to frivolous entertainment, or other similar things about which disagreement [among scholars as to permissibility] exists, then he should be left to his state and to his Lord, this is by way of choosing safety and avoiding denial of that of which one has no thorough knowledge. For God has secrets of His own in his creation. "*Your Lord has more knowledge of you, if He will He will show mercy on you and if He will He will punish you, and We sent you not as a custodian over them.*" [17:84] And God knows best.

We have dictated these few words concerning these questions, as they bear elaboration although clear. We ask God for forgiveness, rely on Him, and seek His protection against the evil in ourselves and that in our deeds. "*Transcendent are You! We have no knowledge saving that which You have taught us, You are The Knowing, The Wise.*" [2:32]

Dictation ended in Dhul-Qa'da, one of the forbidden months[75] of the year 1125. May God bless our lord Muḥammad, his House and Companions, and grant them peace.

GLOSSARY

A

Abdāl: plural of *badal*. See *badal*.

Adab: Courtesy, good manners, the correct manner of doing something.

Ādāb: Plural of *adab*.

Adhān: The call to each of the five obligatory ritual prayers.

Afrād: Plural of *fard*. See *fard*.

Ahl: The people of…

Ahl-Allāh: The men of God.

Ahl-al-Bayt: The People of the House, the family of the Prophet, may God's blessings and peace be upon him and them.

Ahl-al-Aḥwāl: Those under the sway of a powerful spiritual state.

Ahl-al-Khaṭwa: The People of the Step. Those saints capable of crossing great distances by simple putting the right foot forwards and saying "*Bismillāh*" (In the Name of God).

Ahl-al-Sunna wal-Jamā'a: The great majority of orthodox Muslims, as distinct from the Shī'a, *Mu'tazilites*, and other minority sects.

Ahl al-Sirr: The people of the Secret. Those saints granted certain spiritual openings of a major nature.

Aqṭāb: Plural of *Quṭb*. See *Quṭb*.

Arbe'īn: Forty. *Al-Arbe'īn al-Aṣl*, The Forty Principles: Title of a book by Imām al-Ghazālī.

Arbe'īniyya: The forty days retreat of the Sufis.

Arwāḥ: plural of *rūḥ*. See *rūḥ*.

Aṣl: Origin, root, principle.

Awliyā': plural of *walī*. See *walī*.

Awrād: plural of *wird*. See *wird*.

Awtād: plural of *watad*. There are four in the Circle of Saints, each of who is responsible for one of the four cardinal directions.

'A

'Ābid: Worshipper, devotee.

'Ābidūn or *'Ābidīn*: Plural of *'Ābid*.

'Ālam: A world, dimension or level of existence, or a specific part thereof.

'Ālam al-Amr: The World of the Divine Command, sometimes taken to be synonymous with the World of the Spirits.

'Ālam al-Arwāḥ: The World of Spirits.

'Ālam al-Mulk: The physical world or world of dense forms. The lowest in the ternary *Mulk, Malakūt, Jabarūt.*

'Ālam al-Nāsūt: The human element in *'Ālam al-Mulk.*

'Ālam al-Shahāda: The Visible World. Everything perceptible through the five senses. Corollary of *'Ālam al-Ghayb,* which is the unseen.

'Ālam al-Ṣuwar: The World of Forms. Includes both the *Mulk* or World of Dense Forms and the *Malakūt* or World of Subtle Forms.

'Ālam al-Ẓilāl: The World of Shadows, which is the physical world seen as the dense shadows projected by higher realities. It is used to underline the illusory and ephemeral nature of the material level of existence.

'Ālim: Scholar, learned man.

'Ārif: One who knows. For Sufis: Gnostic. He who knows by that direct spiritual perception which transcends sensory and mental knowledge. This is why they call him *'Ārif bil'llāh*, the one who knows by God, not by himself.

'Arīf: Deputy, aid. For Sufis: A rank in the Circle of Saints.

'Aṣr: Late afternoon. An epoch. The mid-afternoon obligatory ritual prayer.

B

Badal: A high ranking member of the Circle of Sainthood by whose *du'ā'* the Muslim community thrives and is protected from various calamities. Their number is forty according to some hadiths and whenever one of them dies he is immediately replaced by another saint.

Basmalah: The utterance: "*Bismillāh*", in the Name of God.

Baraka: Benediction. Spiritual influence. The effect of the higher worlds on the material and psychic planes to cause things to thrive.

Barzakh: That which separates. The intermediary world separating and connecting this world to the world of the resurrection. Also, the intermediary world separating and connecting the material and spiritual dimensions.

Baqā': Subsistence after spiritual extinction.

Bid'a: Innovation, heresy, something that has been introduced into the practice of religion and goes against the recognized principles.

D

Dā'ira: Circle.

Da'wa: Invitation. Summoning the people to answer the Divine call and accept God's invitation to Paradise and His presence.

Dhawq: The sense of taste, also the verb: tasting. This term is used by the Sufis to indicate the immediate perception or experience of higher realities which is as direct as sensory perception.

Dīwān: Collection of poems belonging to a single poet.

Dīwān al Awliyā': The Conference of the Saints.

Dhikr: To remember, or to mention. All kinds of teaching sessions of religious knowledge is called *Dhikr*. For Sufis: The remembrance of God, whether using specific formulas or simply being aware of Him, whether silently or aloud, and whether singly or in congregation.

Du'ā': Calling upon. The word has come to retain only the religious meaning of prayer or supplication.

F

Faqīh: One who understands well. Now used only to designate a jurisprudent, an expert in *sharī'a*.

Faqīr: Poor person. Sufis have taken to calling themselves *faqīr* based on the Qur'ānic verse saying, *"O Mankind, you are the ones that have need of God, He is the All-Sufficient, the Praiseworthy*." [35:15]

Far': Literally: branch of a tree. Also branches of various sciences, as opposed to principles.

Fard: A very high ranking saint thought by some to escape the jurisdiction of the Pole.

Farq: Separation. For Sufis: *al-Farq al awwal*, the first separation, is the veiling of the servant from his Lord by his ordinary consciousness. *Al-Farq al-Thānī*, the second separation, is the return to ordinary consciousness after having achieved reunion and "arrived", then neither creation veils him from the Creator, nor the Creator from creation.

Fatḥ: Opening, victory. *Fatḥ Makka*: The conquest of Makka. For Sufis: any grace received by the traveler to help him overcome the obstacles facing him. *Al-Fatḥ al-Kabīr*: The Major Opening which is the prerogative of the "elect of the elect" and leads to the unveiling of all the worlds, from the material to the Divine.

Fātiḥa: The Opener. The opening *sūra* of the Qur'ān, the recitation of which is obligatory during every single *rak'a* of the ritual prayer. It is also frequently recited to seal prayers and supplications and to be offered to the dead.

Fikr: Reflection.

Fiṭra: The pattern in which a thing was at its origin, at the beginning of its creation, before its modification by the action of time and the environment. The inborn qualities of a being. The original nature of mankind.

Fuqarā': Plural of *faqīr*.

Furū': Plural of *far'*. See *far'*.

Futūḥ or *Futūḥāt*: Plural of *Fatḥ* e.g. *Futūḥ al-Ghayb*, the Openings of the Unseen, a book by Shaykh 'Abdal-Qādir al-Jilānī, and *al-Futūḥāt al-Makkiyya*, by Shaykh ibn 'Arabī.

G

Ghawth: Succor. For the Sufis: The head of the hierarchy of saints, the supreme *Quṭb*.

Ghayba: Absence. For Sufis: the spiritual state of being absent to creation when overwhelmed by the Divine presence.

H

Ḥabīb: Beloved. God's Greatest Beloved, *al-Ḥabīb al-A'ẓam*, is one of the Prophet's names. *Al-Ḥabīb* came to be the title of the Ḥusaynī *sharīfs* of Hadramawt, the Banī-'Alawī *sayyids*, from the 11th century of the *Hijra* onward.

Ḥadīth: Utterance, conversation. *Ḥadīth Nabawī*, Prophetic utterance, the preserved traditions of the Prophet, may God's blessings and peace be upon him. *Hadīth Qudsī*: Holy Tradition; the Divinity speaking by the tongue of the Prophet, may God's blessings and peace be upon him.

Ḥaḍra: Presence. For Sufis the term on its own is used to designate a gathering of *dhikr*. The term qualified may mean the Divine Presence, *al-Ḥaḍra al-Ilāhiyya*, or the Prophet's presence, *al Ḥaḍra al-Muḥammadiyya,* or any other presence.

Ḥajj: The greater Pilgrimage held yearly in the month of *Dhul-Ḥajja*. One of the five pillars of Islam, its various rites are symbols of the traveler's path to the Divine presence.

Ḥāl: Transient spiritual state.

Ḥalāl: Licit, lawful as opposed to *ḥarām*.

Ḥaqīqa: Reality. The inner reality of things which can be perceived only by *kashf* or unveiling.

Ḥaqq: Truth. As a Divine Name it indicated He Who alone truly is, He Who Alone is real.

Ḥaram: Sanctuary, sacred precinct. The two Noble sanctuaries are Makka and Madina.

Ḥarām: Forbidden, illicit.

Ḥawā: Passion, caprice, whim.

Ḥijr: The semicircular enclosure on the northern side of the Ka'ba; it used to be part of the Ka'ba in ancient days and is called *Ḥijr Ismā'īl.*

Hijra: Migration. The *Hijrī* calendar begins with the year of the Prophet's emigration from Makka to Madina.

Ḥizb: A Party of people gathered for a special purpose. A political party. For Sufis: a collection of invocations strung together into a litany.

Himma: Resolution, determination, motivation.

I

'Īd: Feast. There are two main Muslim feasts: The greater one, *'Īd al-Aḍḥā*, celebrating the completion of the *hajj*; and the lesser one, *'Īd al-Fiṭr*, celebrating the completion of the fast of Ramaḍān.

Idhn: Permission, authorization.

Ilbās: To cover or clothe with. For Sufis: the investiture with the *Khirqa*.

Ilhām: Inspiration.

Iḥsān: Thoroughness, excellence. The highest level of the triad mentioned in hadith: *Islām, Īmān, Iḥsān. Islām* corresponds to outward activity and therefore the physical world, the human body, and *sharī'a. Īmān* corresponds to belief and emotional attachment to the tenets of faith, therefore to the subtle world, the human soul and *tarīqa. Ihsān* corresponds to gnosis, therefore to the spiritual world of lights and *ḥaqīqa*.

Ijāza: Permission, authority. The authorization granted by scholars to their students to teach a particular science. For Sufis, 'Alawīs in particular: admission to the path, permission to recite certain *awrād* or perform certain practices.

'Ilm: Knowledge, science.

'Ilm ladunnī: Inward knowledge of inspiration or unveiling.

Īmān: Faith, belief. See *Iḥsān*.

Imām: Leader, leading authority.

Iqāma: The second announcement for each of the five daily prayers. The first announcement, the *adhān*, calls people to the mosque, allowing them time to perform their *wuḍū'*. The second announcement or *iqāma* is made immediately before the *takbīr* heralding that the prayer has begun.

Irāda: Desire, wish, decision, will. For Sufis: The determination to be a *murīd* and travel the path.

Irshād: Guidance, counseling.

'Ishā': The fifth ritual prayer of the day taking place approximately ninety minutes after sunset.

Islām: To surrender or submit; see *Iḥsān*. Also the name Divinely ascribed to all revealed religions, therefore most suitable for the last revelation which embraces and completes all previous ones.

Ittiḥād: Union. The union of two separate entities into a single new one. Sufis are accused by their detractors of claiming of themselves union with God. They reply that this is a logical impossibility since the Infinite cannot possibly unite with the finite and since God is not another "entity" to unite with. The technical term they use for union is *Jam'* which means that the finite may lose its own separative consciousness of itself and become conscious only of the Infinite. The finite does not thereby lose its existence by uniting with the Infinite, but only its ordinary consciousness of itself.

J

Jabarūt: Immense power. *'Ālam al- Jabarūt,* the World of Power. The term means different things to different schools of Sufis. It is sometimes used to indicate the World of the Spirit, the highest created world.

Jadhb: Pull, attraction. For Sufis: the Divine pull that overpowers the seeker and takes him up to the Divine Presence, helping him overcome the downward pull of his earthy appetites and passions. It usually comes after he has achieved adequate preparation, rarely as a pure grace without prior preparation.

Jam': union. See *Ittiḥād.*

Jawāz: Permission, crossing over.

Jawāziyya: The *khirqa jawāziyya* signifies the admission of the seeker as a traveler on the path, signaling thereby that he has crossed the boundary separating the stationary seekers of *baraka* from the actual travelers.

Jihād: Struggle, battle. The lesser *Jihād, al jihād al-asghar* is the military battle against infidel invaders. The Greater *Jihād, al jihād al-akbar*, is the spiritual struggle against the dark aspects of the soul to release it from its earthly shackles and allow it to soar up to its Lord. It is the Greater *Jihād* because it is a relentless struggle that allows for no rest and no distraction, whereas military *jihād* is confined to physical battlefields which are limited.

Jinn: These beings made of the element fire and usually invisible to the physical eye. Some are Muslims and some not.

K

Karāma: To honor, to treat with generosity. For Sufis: supernatural events wrought by saints, the miracles of saints not prophets. The extra-ordinary happenings *(Kharq al-'āda)* by which God confirms, supports and reassures the elect.

Karāmāt: plural of *karāma.*

Kashf: Unveiling. For Sufis: the opening of the inward eye that perceives the subtle domain.

Khalīfa: Deputy, successor. The *Khalīfa* is the one who stands in for someone else, which means he must be qualified and invested with the power to shoulder his responsibilities to the full. The position or function of the *Khalīfa* is called *al-Khilāfa.* The most precise term for *Khalīfa* would be vicar, were it not for its current connotations. God's first *Khalīfa* on earth was Adam. The Prophet's *Khalīfa* is his successor at the head of the Islamic state (Caliph) so long as he upholds the sacred law. As for Sufi orders, the term *Khalīfa* is used to designate either the master's deputy or his successor.

Khalwa: Spiritual retreat whereby a Sufi traveler secludes himself entirely, apart from attending congregational prayers, and devotes himself to concentrated remembrance of God in order to force a spiritual result within a specified period.

Khawārīj: The heretic rebels who assassinated the third and fourth Rightly-Guided Caliphs. Their mark is that they apply the Qur'ānic verses condemning idolaters and polytheists to the Muslims, denounce them as *kāfirs*, then have no qualms in killing them. Today's *khawārij* are those who believe that difference of opinion within the Muslim community is forbidden, that anyone who holds views different from their own is a *kāfir* and destined for Hell, and that they, although an absolute minority, are the only ones to go to paradise, whereas the remaining twelve billion Muslims are not Muslims at all.

Khidr: This is the popular form of the word, the correct spelling being *Khadir*, which means green. *Al-Khidr*, or al-*Khadir* is the hidden master of the Gnostic saints. He appears in the Qur'ān in *sūra al-Kahf* as the teacher of hidden realities to Moses. The Sufis maintain that he is still around and that they see and learn from him.

Khirqa: small piece of cloth. For Sufis: whatever item of clothing a master may invest the disciple with.

Khilāfa: Vice regency, succession. See *Khalīfa*.

Kufr: Disbelief, infidelity. Literally, to cover something up. The disbeliever is a *kāfir*.

L

Labbayk: The Muslim's answer when called, it means: "Yes! I am here listening and willing to obey."

M

Madad: Reinforcement, supply. Reinforcing an army with men, increasing someone's wealth or children, and so on. For Sufis: reinforcing the traveler with assistance from the spiritual world.

Maghrib: Sunset. The sunset obligatory ritual prayer.

Mahdī: Rightly guided. The Leader promised to save the Muslims at the end of time when corruption and evil have reached their maximum. There are dozens of Prophetic traditions describing him and his function.

Maḥfūẓ: Protected, guarded. The Guarded Tablet is *al-Lawḥ al-Mahfūẓ*. Upon it has the Divine Pen inscribed all that is to happen from the beginning of creation to the Resurrection. It is guarded against interference and against unauthorized eyes.

Majdhūb: One who is being pulled. For Sufis: an ecstatic; a man so powerfully attracted by the higher worlds that he loses his earthside consciousness or part thereof.

Mala': Assembly or conference of high ranking people, the eminent or influential members of a community. *Al-Mala' al-A'lā,* the Highest or Supreme Assembly consists of the archangels responsible for the universe.

Malāmatī: A Saint whose spiritual station is high but who shows no outward sign of it, his observable behavior being ordinary to the extreme. Although often confused with them, they are different from *ahl al-Takhrīb*, those who exhibit behavior that seemingly breaks the sacred law.

Malakūt: See *'Ālam al-Malakūt*.

Manāf: An ancestor of the Prophet was called 'Abd Manāf, thus the House of Manāf is the House of the Prophet.

Ma'rifa: Knowledge, information. For Sufis: gnosis, that knowledge which is directly perceived by the eye of the heart and which pertains to the Divine Acts, names and Attributes. In that respect it is higher than *kashf* or unveiling.

Mawlid: Birth. Prose or poetry compositions celebrating the Prophet's birth and recited in gatherings which are themselves also called *mawlids*.

Miḥrāb: The prayer niche where the *Imām* stands to lead the ritual prayer in the mosque.

Minā: The valley between 'Arafāt and Makka where the pilgrims camp for the three *'Īd* days following the day of 'Arafāt.

Minhāj: Method, technique. *Al Minhāj* is a famous book of advanced Shāfi'ī *fiqh* by Imām al-Nawawī.

Mi'rāj: Ladder, ascent. *Laylat'al-Mi'rāj* is the night the prophet was taken up through the *Malakūt*, beyond the Throne, and into the Divine presence.

Mu'azzin: The man who announce the five daily prayers by calling the *adhān* from the minaret.

Mu'jiza: Miracle, supernatural or extra-ordinary event wrought at the hands of a Divine Envoy. If at the hands of a saint it will be called a *karāma*.

Mufassir: Qur'ānic exegete or commentator.

Muḥaḍara: God's imposed awareness of Him on Those whom He chooses, until such time that they are given the Opening.

Muḥaddith: Traditionist, expert on *ḥadith*.

Mu'jiza: Miracle confirming Divine Messengers.

Mujaddid: Renewer.

Mujtahid: Striver, one who relies upon his own effort or *ijtihād*. In *sharī'*, an independent scholar capable of deriving the rulings of *sharī'a* directly from the Qur'ān and *Sunna*, rather than following any other authority such as the founder of any of the four schools.

Mukāshafa: Unveiling. See *Kashf*.

Mulk: Kingdom. See *'Ālam al-Mulk*.

Multazam: That portion of the wall of the Ka'ba that is beneath its door and South of it to the Black Stone. Pilgrims cling to it in the knowledge that this is one location where prayers are sure to be answered.

Munāfiq: Hypocrite.

Muqallid: Followers of a particular school of jurisprudence. A scholar who has not reached the stage of *ijtihād*. See also *mujtahid*.

Muqaddam: One who has been given prominence or leadership. *Al-Faqīh al-Muqaddam*: The Foremost Jurisprudent, title of Imām Muḥammad ibn 'Alī Bā-'Alawī. For certain Sufis, but not for 'Alawīs, the *muqaddam* is the *Shaykh's* deputy.

Murīd: Aspirant, one who desires something. For Sufis: the seeker of truth, the disciple who aspires for gnosis.

Muṣafaḥa: Shaking hands. For Sufis: The shaking of hands. The Shaykh takes the disciple's hand saying: "I shake your hand as Shaykh so and so shook mine." The chain of transmission thus rises up unbroken to the Prophet (may God's blessings and peace be upon him), who had bid his Companions shake each others' hands in greeting, rather than embracing or bowing to each other. This has nothing to do with the Sufi pact of allegiance. It may also mean kissing the Shaykh's hand.

Mushāhada: Contemplation. The direct vision of the Divine Names, Attributes and Acts. The real goal of the path.

Mutajarrid: One who has divested himself from all worldly possessions.

Mutaṣawwif: One who has entered the Sufi path but not yet reached the stage of being a Sufi. A serious seeker as opposed to the *muṣtaṣwif* who imitates the Sufis outwardly with no serious intention of following their path.

Muzdalifa: The valley separating 'Arafāt from Minā. On leaving 'Arafāt the pilgrims have to spend the night there or at least stop for a while before proceeding to Minā.

N

Najīb: Excellent, remarkable. For Sufis: A rank in the Circle of Saints.

Naqīb: Group leader or representative. For Sufis: A rank in the Circle of Saints.

Nafs: Soul, psyche, ego, self. The subtle form of a human being which is the transitional level between the luminous spirit and the dense body.

Nasā'iḥ: Plural of *naṣīḥa*: counsel.

Nujabā': Plural of *Najīb*.

Nuqabā': Plural of *Naqīb*.

Q

Qaḍā': Divine decree, the Divine decision in the pre-existing Divine knowledge.

Qadar: The execution of the decree in its predestined time and mode.

Qalb: Heart

Qawī: Strong, mighty.

Qawm: The People, the Folk. This is what the Sufis call themselves, based on the *ḥadith* which describes the circles of remembrance and the descent of the angels upon them and ends with, "they are the people whose companions never suffer wretchedness."

Qaylūla: The midday nap preceding the *Ẓuhr* prayer which was the Prophet's *Sunna*.

Quṭb: Pole, center of a circle, wheel, or sphere. For Sufis: the *Quṭb* is the supreme authority in each town, territory, or spiritual state. The Pole of Poles, *Quṭb al-Aqṭāb*, is *al-Ghawth*, the Succor.

R

Rābiṭa: Bond. For Sufis: The inward intellectual and emotional attachment of a disciple to his Shaykh.

Rajul: Man. For Sufis: a man true to his Adamic nature, that is one who has achieved the completion of virtue.

Rak'a: Unit of ritual prayer consisting in the recitation of the *Fātiḥa* and some others parts of the Qur'ān while standing, followed by one bow and two prostrations.

Ribāṭ: Perseverance, continual performance of a function. To stand guard during wartime. To remain in a state of ritual purity in readiness for one ritual prayer after another. For 'Alawīs the *ribāṭ* is a school for religious sciences.

Risāla: Epistle, letter, treatise.

Riā': Ostentation, to perform a devotional act in public not for the sake of God but for other people to witness it.

Rijāl: Men. Plural of *rajul*. *Rijāl al-Ghayb*: Men of the Unseen, saints whose function is hidden from ordinary eyes.

Riyāḍa: Taming, training, disciplining.

Rubūbiyya: Lordship.

Rūḥ: Spirit.

Ru'yā: Vision, usually dream vision.

S

Sāda: Plural of *sayyid*. See *sayyid*.

Salām: Peace. *Al-Salām* is a Divine Attribute. Greeting with the formula: *"Al-Salāmu 'alaykum!"* (May peace be upon you!) which is the specifically Muslim way of greeting taught by the Prophet, may God's blessings (*ṣalāt*) and peace (*salām*) be upon him.

Ṣalāt: Prayer.

Salb: Dispossession.

Ṣāliḥ: Virtuous, a person well established in the behavior most pleasing to God.

Samā': Audition, spiritual concert.

Sayyid: Master, lord. The term is used to designate the descendants of the Prophet through Imām Ḥasan or Imām Ḥusayn. The form *sayyidunā* means "our master".

Shādhili: An affiliate of the Shādhilī Sufi order founded by Imām Abul-Ḥasan al-Shādhilī.

Shāfi'ī: A follower of the Shāfi'ī school of jurisprudence founded by Imām Muḥammad ibn Idrīs al-Shāfi'ī.

Shahāda: Witnessing, testimony; the two *shahādas* are *lā ilāha illa'llāh, Muḥammadun Rasūlu'llāh*. Also see *'ālam al-shahāda*.

Sharī'a: Islamic sacred law.

Sharīf: Nobleman. A descendant of the Prophet.

Shaykh: Old man. For Sufis: the master of an order. For the various meanings of the word shaykh, see: "Key to the Garden" by *Ḥabīb* Aḥmad Mashhūr al-Ḥaddād, p. 124.

Shī'a: Heterodox Muslim minority who believe that the Caliphate belonged by right to Imām 'Alī and consequently criticize the other Companions. There are two main sects of *Shī'a*: the Twelver *Shī'as* of Iran and Iraq and the Zaydī *Shī'a* of northern Yemen.

Ṣiddīq: Utterly veracious. For Sufis: the highest degree of sanctity.

Sirr: Secret. For Sufis: the Divinely bestowed special attribute or attributes that allow saints and spiritual masters to carry out their functions. Also: the highest element in the hierarchy comprising the body, soul, spirit and secret.

Ṣubḥ: Morning. In *sharī'a*: same as *fajr*, the dawn ritual prayer.

Sukr: Drunkenness, intoxication. Also see *ghayba* and *jadhb*.

Sulūk: Traveling. A traveler is a *sālik*.

Sunna: Pattern of behavior. In *sharī'a*: the words and deeds of the Prophet, may God's blessings and peace be upon him.

Sunnī: One who belongs to *Ahl al-Sunna wal-Jamā'a*, i.e an orthodox Muslim. The term has been used abusively by fundamentalist groups who claim to be the true followers of the *Sunna* and accuse the great majority of Muslims of overt heresy.

Sūra: Chapter of the Qur'ān of which there are one hundred and fourteen.

T

Tafsīr: Qur'ānic exegesis or commentary.

Taḥkīm: Total authority. The old pattern of Sufism whereby the master required that the disciple surrender unconditionally to his authority. This method is unsuitable for today's disciples who have neither the power of certitude nor the spiritual resolution to sustain such training.

Tā'iyya: Poem in *tā'*.

Talwīn: Changing color. For Sufis: the changes that appear on the traveler under the influence of successive states.

Tamkīn: Mastery, firm establishment. No changes appear on the master who dominates his spiritual states rather than being dominated by them.

Taqwā: The fear of God. To act in the constant awareness of His presence.

Ṭarīqa: A particular way or method of doing something. For Sufis: the technique, whether outward or inward, particular to each order. By extension, the order itself.

Tawba: Repentance.

Tawḥīd: Unification. *Shahādat'al-tawḥīd*: the Testimony of Divine Unity, *lā ilāha illa'llāh*. Unification is to acknowledge only one Divinity and to unify all one's abilities and emotions into the single minded pursuit of nearness to that Divinity.

U

'Ubūda: This is a term coined by the Sufis to designate the state of total slavehood. It is the highest degree in the triad: *'Ibāda*: worshiping God. *'Ubūdiyya*: being a thorough servant of God inwardly by remaining serene and content throughout whatever tests or hardships He has chosen to impose and by renouncing desire for anything that differs from His will. *'Ubūda*: having no will other than that of God.

'Ubūdiyya: Servitude. See above.

Uns: Intimate satisfaction, inward comfort. For Sufis: a spiritual state brought about by the unveiling of the Divine Attributes of Beauty, which makes it the expansive corollary of the contraction brought about by the unveiling of the Divine Attributes of Majesty and termed *Hayba*, awe.

'Urafā': Plural of *'Arīf.*

Uṣūl: Plural of *Aṣl*. See *Aṣl*. The sciences of *Uṣul* comprise that of the Principles of Beliefs, in which context *Uṣūl* will mean beliefs and *furū'* (branches or applications) will mean jurisprudence; and that of the Principles of Jurisprudence, *Uṣul al-Fiqh*, in which case it will mean the science of reaching a legal ruling as distinct from jurisprudence which is that of the legal rulings themselves.

'Uẓla: Isolation. In Sufi terms, it means that one isolates oneself from the community, not totally as in Khalwa or retreat, but partially so as to be able to devote oneself to worship and study without distraction.

W

Walī: Protégé, ally, close friend, supporter, also governor, caretaker. "*God is the* Walī *of those who believe*", says the Qur'ān [2:257]. All believers are *awliyā'* in the general acceptance of the term since they have chosen God for their protector and ally. For Sufis: a *walī* is he whom God has taken under his special protection and enveloped in his solicitude, eventually to elevate him into His presence.

Wara': Scrupulousness, circumspection.

Wārid: Something that arrives, a sudden inspiration or spiritual state, the inward result of an act of worship.

Wāridāt: Plural of *Wārid*.

Watad: Pillar, For Sufis: A rank in the Circle of Saints.

Wilāya: The attribute of the *walī*.

Wird: A regular devotional function.

Wuḍū': Ritual ablutions.

Wujūd: Existence.

Y

Ya-Sīn: The thirty sixth *sūra* of the Qur'ān said by the Prophet to be the "heart of the Qur'ān". Also one of the Prophet's names.

Z

Zakāt:The obligatory tax paid yearly as an act of worship by any Muslim possessing over a *niṣāb* or minimum requirement in money, crops, cattle or commercial goods. It is one of the five pillars of Islam.

Zaydī: The *Shī'a* sect of Northen Yemen who claim to have originated with Imām Zayd grandson of Imām Ḥusayn.

Ẓuhr: Noon. The midday ritual prayer.

NOTES

1. *Ṣiddīqūn*: Plural of *ṣiddīq*, the highest rank in sainthood and thus that of those immediately below the rank of Prophethood. See glossary.

2. A master is he who has achieved mastery over a certain activity, whether it be training a human being or an animal, disposing of a certain domain, or excelling in a craft or a science.

3. The contemplative is he who is following a spiritual path and moving through its stages to reach that stage where knowledge comes from inspiration, or direct vision of the hidden reality through the Eye of the Heart.

4. The word 'entrenched' here means that they have dug into their positions and are holding them with tenacity.

5. Imām Aḥmad ibn Zayn al-Ḥabashī was a well known scholar and author of encyclopedic learning, a high ranking saint, and the foremost student and successor of Imām al-Ḥaddād. He died in 1144 A.H.

6. Al-Tumbuktī means that he originally hailed from Timbuktu in Mali.

7. The "Faction" here indicates the Sufi;, it means something much more akin to a "group" and has no sectarian implications.

8. The correct pronunciation of this name is: al-Khadir, as the Prophet (may God's blessings and peace be upon him) is known to have pronounced, as in the *ḥadith* of Bukhārī. However, we have opted for the more familiar manner in which people including scholars have been pronouncing it for centuries, which is: al-Khidr

9. What the Imām means by discourses here amounts to no more than brief indications or allusions, for he never discoursed at length on any such subject, except perhaps in his private sessions with Imām Aḥmad ibn Zayn al-Ḥabashī and other gnostic disciples.

10. Solicitude in this context means Divine protection, guidance, provision, and comfort.

11. *Uṣūl*, refer to glossary.

12. "*And when Moses came to Our appointed time and his Lord spoke with him, he said, 'O my Lord, show me, that I may behold You!' He said, 'You shall not see Me; but behold the mountain, if it stays fast in its place, then you shall see Me.' And when his Lord revealed Himself to the mountain He made it crumble to dust; and Moses fell down swooning*." Qur'ān [7:143]

13. The mind thinks in abstract terms.

14. The imagination operates with images.

15. Gnosis is direct knowledge, transcending both the cognitive and imaginative levels, pertaining to the spirit, not the soul.

16. See glossary for explanation of Arabic terms.

17. The rights of Lordship are: to conform to the sacred law outwardly, maintain constant presence of heart inwardly, and courtesy with created beings.

18. Suffering, being wronged, and forgiving those who have committed that wrong are major pathways to God's forgiveness. God reforms those corrupt persons he wishes to attract into His mercy by testing them with painful trials, then inspiring them with patience, contentment and forgiveness.

19. None knows God so as to praise Him as He deserves to be. Only He knows Himself and only He, in His revealed Scriptures, can praise Himself adequately.

20. "Those who are too occupied with the remembrance of Me to ask Me for anything, I shall give them better than that which I give those who ask." (*Ḥadith Qudsi*)

21. This *hadith* indicates that standing as a destitute supplicant before God, acknowledging His Sovereignty and Generosity, is the essence of all forms of worship.

22. When God 'takes' a man, it is to make him a *walī* or protégé of His.

23. A famous book by Shaykh Ibn 'Atā'illāh of Alexandria about the life, states, knowledge and supernatural events of his shaykh, Abu'l-'Abbās al-Mursī and his master Shaykh Abul-Ḥasan al-Shādhilī, (may God sanctify their secrets).

24. A book by Imām al-Suyūṭī detailing the conditions of the Intermediary Realm (*al-Barzakh*), the world where the dead await the resurrection.

25. A sinister end to a life is for the heart to swerve away from faith so that the person dies a disbeliever.

26. The passage runs as follows: "We shall clarify these degrees with the example that your believing that Zayd is in the house having three levels. The first is that you are so informed by someone whom you know by experience is truthful, not a liar, and whose words you have never doubted. Your heart trusts him and has confidence in what he says just because he has said it. This is "belief by following" which resembles that of the common people who, when they reached the age of discrimination, hear from their fathers and mothers of the existence of God the Exalted, His knowledge, will, ability, as well as His other

Attributes. [They also hear] that messengers were sent, were truthful and [they hear of] their message. Whatever they hear they accept with firmness and confidence. It does not cross their minds that things might be different from what they were told since they think well of their fathers, mothers and teachers. This faith results in salvation in the hereafter, those who possess it are foremost among the "Companions of the Right Hand", but they are not of the "Foremost" since it lacks unveiling, insight, and the expansion of the breast with the light of certitude. Error is possible in transmission, both in the case of single chains and that of multiple chains, in what concerns beliefs. The hearts of the Jews and Christians are also confident in what they hear from their fathers and mothers. However, what they hear is wrong and consequently their beliefs are wrong. Similarly Muslims believe the truth not because they see it but because it is told to them.

The second level is for you to hear the voice of Zayd and his words from the house but from behind the wall; you will conclude that he is in the house but your belief, acceptance, and certainty that he is in the house will be much stronger than from mere hearsay. Thus if you are told that he is in the house, then you hear his voice, your certainty increases, for sounds indicate forms and bodies for whoever has heard the voice while witnessing the body. His heart then concludes that this voice belongs to that person. This is faith mixed with evidence. Here also error is possible, for a voice may resemble another, it may even be deliberately imitated which may not occur to the hearer if he suspects no such trickery and never thought of a motive to cause it.

The third level is to enter the house, see him with your own eyes and look at him. This is real knowledge, the vision that is certain and which resembles that of the "Drawn Near" and the *Ṣiddīqūn*, for their faith is based on direct vision, therefore the faith of the common people and that of the theologians is encompassed by theirs and they surpass them by a special attribute which makes error impossible. They also differ in the amount of knowledge and degree of unveiling.

As for the degrees of unveiling, the example is seeing Zayd at close range in the courtyard of the house in broad daylight; the perception is then perfect. Or seeing him inside the house or at a distance or in the evening, he is thus seen to be him of a certainty, but this seeing lacks the previous clarity of vision and perception of minute details. The same thing may be imagined to apply to the contemplation (*mushāhada*) of Divine matters.

As for the abundance of knowledge, it is as if he sees in the house Zayd, 'Umar and Bakr while another sees only Zayd. The knowledge of the first inevitably increases with the increase of information.

This is the state of the heart as concerns knowledge; God knows better what is right." *Iḥyā' Ulūm al-Din*, Dār al-Ma'rifa, Beirut 1982. pp. 15-16.

27. "*Kitāb Sharḥ 'Ajā'ib al-Qalb*", (The Book that Explains the Marvels of the Heart).

28. This refers to the *ḥadith*: "The world is accursed and accursed is what is in it, except enjoining good, forbidding evil and remembering God."

29. Abū 'Alī al-Rūdhbārī is one of the famous 4th century Sufis mentioned by Qushayrī in his treatise. The verses in question read as follows:

They said: Tomorrow is the Feast, what will you wear?
　　I said: The gift of a pourer whose love I have quaffed
Poverty and fortitude are the two garments beneath which
　　is a heart beholding its comfort in Feasts and Fridays
No garb is more suited to meet the Beloved in
　　on visiting day than the garment He has bestowed
Time passes in mourning in Your absence, O my hope!
　　The Feast is when You are to be seen to me and heard.

30. This is a *ḥadith qudsī* that runs as follows: "Whoever is hostile to a *walī* of Mine, I declare war on him. My servant draws near to Me with nothing dearer to Me than what I have imposed upon him. My servant continues to draw closer to Me until I love him. And when I love him I become the eye with which he sees, the ear with which he hears, the hand with which he grasps, and the foot with which he walks."

31. God.

32. "*Ṣallū 'alayhi wa sallimū taslīmā*" (invoke blessings upon him and greet him with peace in a resolute and complete manner!)

33. A coin of insignificant value.

34. See "The Lives of Man", chapter 4.

35. Full title: "Treatise on the Good Manners of the Spiritual Disciple's Wayfaring." See *Two Treatises: Mutual Reminding and Good Manners*. Starlatch Press 2002."

36. Al-Zaydī means that this scholar belonged to the Zaydī *Shī'a* of North Yemen. Apart form the usual differences between the *Ahl-al-Sunna* majority and the *Shī'a* concerning the succession of the Prophet (may God's blessings and peace be upon him), the Zaydīs also hold the *mu'tazilite* belief that the acts of creatures originate in them, believing God cannot create the act in the creature then reward or punish it for it.

37. The day that battle broke out between 'Alī, Commander of the Faithful, and his supporters, and the Companions who had quarreled

with him over revenge for 'Uthmān's assassination. Thus called because of the presence of the Mother of the Faithful, the lady 'Ā'isha on her camel.

38. Ṣiffīn is the location where the battle between 'Alī and the people of Syria led by Mu'āwiya took place. Trickery from the Syrians and treachery from those of 'Alī's supporters who became the *Khawārij* led to the battle ending in stalemate.

39. The 'people of decision' are those people whose opinions are sought for the making of crucial decisions and who represent the heads of the Muslim community. During the early Caliphate these were the Companions who had fought with the Prophet at Badr.

40. i.e. May God treat them with rigor rather than with the mercy with which He treats lesser transgressors.

41. Ḥassān ibn Thābit: A companion famous for his ability to improvise powerful poetry. The Blessed Prophet used to say: "God supports Ḥassān with the Holy Spirit," and he used to place a pulpit for him in the mosque from which he used to reply to the disbelievers' verbal attacks most effectively.

42. *Islām* here means the outward acts of worship while *Īmān* refers to all that pertains to the heart.

43. This means that the contemplative vision of the Divine Act manifesting in every creature does not abolish the acknowledgement that what *sharī'a* declares to be good is to be approved and what it declares to be reprehensible to be reproved.

44. *Khilla* is the special attribute of Abraham whose title is *al-Khalīl* (The Intimate Friend), *Kalām* is the special attribute of Moses who is *al-Kalīm* (He Who Is Spoken To), *Rūḥiyya* is the special attribute of Jesus who is *Rūḥ Allāh* (The Spirit of God), *Maḥbūbiyya* is the special attribute of Muḥammad who is *Ḥabīb Allāh* (The Beloved of God).

45. Dhul-Qarnayn is the mysterious conqueror of old whose story is related in *Sūrat al-Kahf.* He was the man with the two horns who reached the eastern and western confines of the earth and built the barrier keeping Gog and Magog from mankind. *Sūrat al-Kahf*, the chapter of the Cave, is mostly concerned with matters of the unseen or the occurrence of extraordinary events due to the effect of the unseen on the material world. It begins with the sleepers in the cave, mentions how a man's blasphemy attracted revenge from the higher worlds, and contains part of the story of Adam with the Devil, followed by the three strange episodes of al-Khidr with Moses and finally Dhul-Qarnayn.

46. The passage in question is one of the passages from the Shaykh's letters appended to the book. It runs as follows: "The Presence be-

comes the nesting place of their hearts, to it they head for refuge and in it they dwell. Then, when they descend to the heavens of obligations or the earth of allotted shares, they do so with permission, mastery, and deeply rooted certitude. They do not descend to obligations with discourtesy or distraction, nor to allotted shares with passionate appetites or pleasures, rather they engage in them by God, for God, from God, and to God."

The commentary of Shaykh al-Sharnūbī (d.1929 C.E.) on this passage runs as follows: "'*The Presence becomes the nesting place of their hearts, in it they seek refuge and in it they dwell.*' This means that the Presence has become to their hearts as the nest is to the bird. Their state is likened to that of the bird, since to the Presence they go for refuge. There they realize the station of extinction and effacement (*maḥw*) which is the station of union where ends their wayfaring to the Real Sovereign. Following this, they will realize the station of subsistence and sobriety (*saḥw*), which is the station of separation where they are ordered to mix with the people. This is what is meant by his saying: '*Then, when they descend to the heavens of obligations*,' which are what God imposes on them in their mixing with people. The common attribute of both [heavens and obligations] is that they are difficult to climb up to. '*...or the earth of allotted shares*,' which are the things they desire for themselves to manage their daily lives. These are likened to the earth for the common attribute of their being easy to rest on, '*They do so with permission, mastery, and deeply rooted certitude. They do not descend to obligations with discourtesy or distraction, nor to allotted shares with passionate appetites or pleasures, rather they engage in them by God, for God, from God, and to God.*' Which means that they descend by Divine permission to guide the people with the light that shines in their hearts, which He makes a sign for them, and with mastery in the station of subsistence so that they possess the strength to mix with people and endure their injuries. This can be only after they become firmly established in certainty in God the Exalted. Thus, they do not descend to obligations with bad manners and unawareness of God, but with complete courtesy with people and perfect consciousness in contemplating the Real. For they behold God in everything they see, so that when someone harms them they bear it for the sake of God, his Creator. They see that he was only given power over them by their Lord, because of some sin they committed that is unworthy of them. When someone honors them, they thank him, aware that He who moved his heart to honor them is their Lord. They do not descend to their destined shares with the appetites of the soul nor its pleasures, as would be the aim of those possessed of base souls, but they engage in all this, obligations and shares, by God's help [not creation's], aware of Him at every instant [acting for His sake], taking from Him [not from creation], pleading to Him. Meditate upon this!"

47. The "remaining ones" are the last to have followed in the footsteps of their ancestors in a thorough manner and to have achieved their states and stations and received their heritage of knowledge.

48. The *Malāmatiyya* appeared in Nishapur in the second half of the third century of the *Hijra*. Their specific attribute was that they concentrated on freeing the soul, which they perceived by definition as evil, from all its ailments and imperfections, discoursing at great length on these, rather than on the praiseworthy attributes others strove to acquire. They were called the "People of Blame" because they blamed themselves for both their sins and their acts of worship, the first for obvious reason and the second for their lack of sincerity in performing them. This is why they were so keen to hide them from everyone else's eyes. Abū-Ḥafs of Nishapur described them thus: "The People of Blame are people who live with the Real - Exalted is He! - by guarding their moments [from distraction and idleness] and watching their inward. They blame themselves for every devotion or act of worship that is seen from them, they allow people to witness only their ugly attributes, but hide their good ones. People thus blame them for what they outwardly show, while they blame themselves for what they know they inwardly are. God then honors them with the unveiling of secrets, the knowledge of many kinds of unseen things, and the appearance of *karāmāt* on them. They hide what God the Exalted gives them and continue to appear as they were in the beginning when they blamed their souls, contradicted them, and allowed people to perceive of them only what would repel them, thus keeping them away and averting any threat to their state with God."

49. See glossary.

50. Al-Waḥṭ is a town in South Yemen.

51. The *muqallid* (follower) as opposed to the *mujtahid* (independent scholar) is he who follows someone else in his beliefs and practice of *sharīʻa*, while the *mujtahid* is he who is able to formulate his own belief and practice directly from the Book and *Sunna* and thus becomes an *imām* that others, who are unable to do so, follow.

52. The beginning of religion is how the Prophet was born in Makka, received the Qur'ānic revelation, called his people to Islam and was persecuted until forced to emigrate to Madina.

53. The Prophet accepted from simple bedouin the most elemental statement of beliefs, that there is no god but the One God, High above

all creation, and that Muḥammad is His Messenger, to be obeyed in what he enjoins and forbids on behalf of his Lord.

54. *Mutawātir*: transmitted by a large number of people incapable of being accused of lying or forgery, through numerous different chains of transmission.

55. *Ma'rifa*: This term is usually used by the sufi to indicate gnosis, the direct knowledge of contemplation and unveiling. However, here the *Imām* starts by using the term in its original, wider sense of knowledge, then proceeds to the technical meaning of the Sufis which is gnosis.

56. Unveiling (*kashf* or *mukāshafa*) usually refers to everything seen with the eye of the heart, whether uncreated or created, whereas contemplation (*mushāhada*) usually refers to the Divine Attributes and Acts, not to the created unseen. Unveiling is thus more general and includes the particular mode termed contemplation. However, some Sufis use the terms loosely and sometimes even reverse the meaning.

57. Having defined the difference between the two concepts of unveiling and contemplation, the Imam, just as he did for knowledge and love, refrains from pronouncing on which of the two is superior to the other.

58. *Ḥadith*.

59. Part of a *ḥadith*.

60. i.e., events in the physical world of forms. These events manifest the existence and laws of the physical world and influence it according to their nature.

61. This is part of a poem where the Shaykh mentions his father, the elder 'Aydarūs, stating that he was his spiritual master and exemplar.

62. The word *taḥkīm* is used for the oath of allegiance administered by the master to a would be disciple. The latter by accepting it commits himself entirely to the master's discretion. Imām al-Ḥaddād discontinued this practice, considering the demands it places on the novice to be unrealistic for the people of his and coming times. He replaced it with a milder form of allegiance which he called *ṭarīqat ahl al-yamīn*.

63. Responsibility. That which makes a man accountable for his actions before God.

64. The ten to whom the Prophet (may God's blessings and peace be upon him) explicitly promised paradise. They were Abū Bakr, 'Umar, 'Uthmān, 'Alī, Talḥa, Zubayr, Sa'd ibn Abī Waqqās, 'Abdal-Raḥmān ibn 'Awf, Sa'īd ibn Zayd, and Abū 'Ubayda ibn al-Jarrāḥ.

65. *Jihād* here is striving to care for the two parents and please them.

66. Again referring to the parents.

67. The complete passage runs as follows: "*There is no fault in those who believe and do deeds of righteousness [regarding] what they may eat, if they are God fearing, believe, and do deeds of righteousness, and then are God fearing and believe, and then are God fearing and do good; God loves those who act with excellence.*"

68. The version in Muslim and Tirmidhī of this *ḥadith* runs as follows: "Forty days, a day as a year, a day as a month, a day as a week, and the rest of his days as yours."

69. Here the *Imām* gives general directions as to how to proceed when two *ḥadiths* seem to contradict each other, rather than focusing specifically on the question at hand.

70. The definitive argument on this matter is that the Prophet (may God's blessings and peace be upon him) as well as the great gnostics among his Companions were all witnessing the eternal Divine will and act that moved them as well as their enemies, whether these were Qurayshī idolaters, Jews or hypocrites. Yet, while witnessing the One Divine Act and Power manifesting in them, they fought many battles against them, behaving towards them as prescribed by *sharī'a.* Mastery in gnosis is to witness God's work in created beings yet treat them strictly according to God's Law.

71. This is a brief pause during the ritual prayer, after the completion of a *rak'a* and before rising to begin another one.

72. The *ḥadith* in full states, "Were God to Judge me and the Son of Mary for what these two have committed, He would punish us without being unjust." Ibn Ḥibbān, *Saḥīḥ,* (659).

73. These are different from the *malāmatīs* with whom they are sometimes confused. The *malāmatī* is a man of high ranking spiritual station who hides it behind a mundane insignificant appearance, while the People of Misbehavior are people who are actually seen to commit acts that outwardly resemble transgressions.

74. The tents indicate the outward acts, manners, and rituals while the women hidden within them indicate the inward spiritual stations, states, and realities.

75. The Pre-Islamic Arabs had four Forbidden Months, three of them surrounding the *Ḥajj* season, *Dhul-Qa'da*, *Dhul-Ḥajja* and *Muḥarram*, and one standing on its own, *Rajab*. During these the usual raids and vendettas were suspended so that pilgrims could travel safely to and from Makka. After the advent of Islam this practice was abrogated but the months still have special *baraka* and certain devotional activities are recommended in them.